# Power of the People Won't Stop:

Legacy of the TWLF at UC Berkeley

A Collection of Writings

**Edited by Harvey Dong, Janie Chen**
Historical photos by Douglas Wachter

Eastwind Books of Berkeley

Power of the People Won't Stop:
Legacy of the TWLF at UC Berkeley

Editor: Harvey Dong
Assistant Editor: Janie Chen
Historical Photos: Douglas Wachter

Copyright © 2019 by Eastwind Books of Berkeley

Published by:
EASTWIND BOOKS OF BERKELEY
2066 University Avenue
Berkeley, CA 94704
www.AsiaBookCenter.com

All rights reserved. No part of this book may be used or reproduced in any manner without written permission from the author and publisher.

Eastwind Books of Berkeley is a registered trademark of Eastwind Books of Berkeley

Published 2020. First Edition
Printed in the United States of America

For more information or to book an author event,
contact www.AsiaBookCenter.com

Front cover photo: Police seal UC campus with TWLF Strike Supporters spilling onto Bancroft and Telegraph. Feb. 20, 1969. Doug Wachter photo.

Back cover photo: TWLF veterans. Photo by Harvey Dong

ISBN: 9781734744002 (paperback)

10 9 8 7 6 5 4 3 2 1

# DEDICATION

This book is about the Third World Liberation Front strike that took place at UC Berkeley in 1969; the solidarity built by peoples of color and their many white allies. It is also about the generations following that have struggle to decolonize the educational system. The story does not end with origins of the struggle. It is very much about the contemporary situation where conditions call for political and social activism, new collective participation and leadership. This multi-generational scope is underscored by the title chosen: "The Power of the People Won't Stop." Narrative reflections and photographs help us to rethink the past, to learn from it, and to become encouraged to change the present.

This work is dedicated to UC Berkeley TWLF 1969, twLF 1999, 2010, 2017... strikers, alumni, teachers, union members, campus staff, students, librarians... those who together make this collective story about solidarity across racial, ethnic and international lines.

# ACKNOWLEDGEMENTS

We are grateful to have on board Douglas Wachter, who worked on campus as a UC Berkeley employee during the time of the 1969 TWLF strike. He supported the strike, took many photographs and preserved them over the years, providing us with important archival material. His photos speak for themselves, expressing the multiracial character of the strike and solidarity that took place.

This book only tells a small part of the story. The original student organizations no longer exist although many new ones have emerged. Many of the early participants have already passed on including Richard Aoki, Alan Fong, Bing Thom and others. 50 years later it is important to acknowledge the collective nature of this movement and the numerous individuals who came together to establish, defend and sustain Ethnic Studies at UC Berkeley and universities nationally.

# TABLE OF CONTENTS

DEDICATION . . . . . . . . . . . . . . . . . . . . . . . . . . . . . . . . . . . . . . . . . . . . . . I
ACKNOWLEDGEMENTS . . . . . . . . . . . . . . . . . . . . . . . . . . . . . . . . . . II
INTRODUCTION: Third World Liberation Comes to San Francisco
   State and UC Berkeley . . . . . . . . . . . . . . . . . . . . . . . . . . . . . . . 1
      *HARVEY DONG*

## CHAPTER ONE: ORIGINS & BACKGROUND

Bandung: The Third World Project . . . . . . . . . . . . . . . . . . . . . . 27
      *JANIE CHEN*
Dr. Carlos Munoz Jr: An Inspiration For All of Us . . . . . . . . . . . . 31
      *PABLO GONZALEZ*
What Happened After I Left the Military . . . . . . . . . . . . . . . . . . 35
      *CARLOS MUNOZ JR*
MASC & the UFW Grape Boycott at Cal . . . . . . . . . . . . . . . . . . 44
      *MANUEL RUBEN DELGADO*
The Wisdom of a College Structure . . . . . . . . . . . . . . . . . . . . . . 53
      *MEXICAN AMERICAN STUDENTS CONFEDERATION (MASC)*
Introduction to "Proposal for Establishing a Black Studies Program" . . 54
      *AFRO-AMERICAN STUDENTS UNION*
Black Panther Party Platform was first to introduce Ethnic Studies
   concept . . . . . . . . . . . . . . . . . . . . . . . . . . . . . . . . . . . . . . . . . 56
Bureau of Indian Affairs (BIA) Relocation Policies . . . . . . . . . . . 57
      *LANADA WAR JACK*
The Student Population to be Served by Indian Studies . . . . . . . . 59
      *UNITED NATIVE AMERICANS*
Understanding AAPA (Asian American Political Alliance) . . . . . . . 61
      *AAPA NEWSPAPER*
Remarks of Prof. Paul Takagi. 1969 . . . . . . . . . . . . . . . . . . . . . . 65
From Asian Studies Proposal. General Purpose and Principles . . . . . 66
      *AAPA*

## CHAPTER TWO: STRIKE REFLECTIONS

Black, Brown, Red, Yellow & White. All the People Must Unite! . . . . 69
      *DOUG WACHTER PHOTOGRAPHY*
The Strike Escalates . . . . . . . . . . . . . . . . . . . . . . . . . . . . . . . . . 85
      *YSIDRO MACIAS*

Joining the TWLF After Relocation . . . . . . . . . . . . . . . . . . . . . . . 90
    *LANADA WAR JACK*

I Am Who I Am Because of the Third World Strike. . . . . . . . . . . . . 94
    *CLEMENTINA DURON*

It's the Peoples University . . . . . . . . . . . . . . . . . . . . . . . . . . . . . . 98
    *CLEMENTINA DURON*

50 Years Later: The Struggle for Social Justice Continues . . . . . . . . .101
    *FLOYD HUEN*

Without Hesitation, I Voted to Strike . . . . . . . . . . . . . . . . . . . . . .103
    *FRANCISCO HERNANDEZ*

Lessons Learned from the Third World Strike . . . . . . . . . . . . . . . .106
    *LILLIAN FABROS*

Video Clip (Poet as Young Revolutionary, Berkeley 1969) . . . . . . . .109
    *JEFFREY THOMAS LEONG*

## CHAPTER THREE: NEW GENERATIONS

Memories of TWLF . . . . . . . . . . . . . . . . . . . . . . . . . . . . . . . . . .117
    *RICKEY VINCENT*

The TWLF Legacy in Immigrant and Refugee Struggles Today . . . . . .122
    *LOAN DAO*

The 1999 twLF Hunger Strike. . . . . . . . . . . . . . . . . . . . . . . . . . .126
    *ROBERTO HERNANDEZ*

African American Studies and the TWLF Strike . . . . . . . . . . . . . . .128
    *ULA TAYLOR*

The Future of Ethnic Studies on its 50th Anniversary: Autonomy
   and Self-Determination Are Missing . . . . . . . . . . . . . . . . . . . .131
    *HARVEY DONG*

What Can Asian American Studies Be? . . . . . . . . . . . . . . . . . . . .135
    *ASIAN AMERICAN STUDIES COALITION AT CAL*

#WhatHappened Campaign: The Current & Future State of AAADS. . .138
    *JACKLIN HA*

School Communities/Community Schools. . . . . . . . . . . . . . . . . .146
    *LAILAN SANDRA HUEN*

Jumping into the River of Justice . . . . . . . . . . . . . . . . . . . . . . . .149
    *KAI NHAM*

We Need to Learn From What Happened . . . . . . . . . . . . . . . . . .151
    *JOANNE YI*

Ethnic Studies Graduation Speech: 50 Means Hope . . . . . . . . . . . .157
    *RIZZA ESTACIO*

## CHAPTER FOUR: CELEBRATING 50 YEARS OF ETHNIC STUDIES

Embracing the Politics of Education: Celebrating 50 Years of Ethnic Studies as a Praxis of Liberation . . . . . . . . . . . . . . . . . . . . . .165
    *ZIZA DELGADO*

BSU/TWLF Veterans Support Arab American Studies (April 2020). . .176

An Ethnic Studies Movement Across California As Never Before . . . .178
    *R. TOLTEKA CUAUHTIN*

Save CA Ethnic Studies Photos . . . . . . . . . . . . . . . . . . . . . .185
    *R. TOLTEKA CUAUHTIN*

Ethnic Studies Historical Legacy . . . . . . . . . . . . . . . . . . . . .191
    *MARIA E. RAMIREZ AND NINA GENERA*

## APPENDIX

Chronology of Events . . . . . . . . . . . . . . . . . . . . . . . . . . .196
    *ABRAHAM RAMIREZ*

Contributors. . . . . . . . . . . . . . . . . . . . . . . . . . . . . . . .206

# INTRODUCTION

## Third World Liberation Comes to San Francisco State and UC Berkeley

HARVEY DONG

*This anthology includes essays, photographs, and reflections from individuals who were involved or influenced by the TWLF strike in 1969 at UC Berkeley. Invitations and announcements were sent out in 2018, one year prior to the TWLF 50th Commemoration at UC Berkeley; and included in this anthology are the responses. This work does not claim to be a complete depiction of what transpired and more needs to be written. Because my life was influenced heavily by the 1969 strike and that I took part in the community work that transpired, I strongly feel that if we do not retell this history, it may be presented inaccurately. Or worse, that it becomes omitted and erased from the narrative of general social movement history. We hear about the importance of struggles such as the Free Speech Movement in 1964 and the People's Park conflict in 1969 but nothing about the role of African Americans, Asian Americans, Native Americans and Mexican Americans to form the TWLF supported by white student allies. The strike reshaped academia then and its legacy has ramifications on how we look at history and societal transformation today. In many ways, the TWLF and the solidarity that emerged has provided future generations to draw on past lessons to struggle, to make change in the present.*

Fifty years have passed since the Third World Liberation Front Strikes led to the establishment of Third World programs that are now called Ethnic Studies. When San Francisco State College students went on strike for Third World Studies, students at the University of California, Berkeley (UCB) moved to support the SF State (SFS) student strikers. They believed then that the best way to express solidarity was to fight for the same demands and principles at UC Berkeley. Another movement front opened at UC Berkeley that had to face similar state repression as at SF State. A strike wave began nationally. The TWLF strikes left imprints for future generations.

The Third World Liberation Strikes that occurred in 1968-9 in the San Francisco Bay Area at San Francisco State (SFS) and the University of California, Berkeley (UCB) had a profound effect on how history is viewed. Firstly, the strikes successfully won civil rights changes in higher education by instituting ethnic studies curriculum and programs. This new approach enabled the study of history to be placed in a comparative context that was focused on looking at institutionalized racism and colonization. Secondly, the strikes caused a significant shift in the mindset of many Third World minority college-aged youth in the San Francisco Bay Area. The post-World War II path towards assimilation into mainstream society from their minority communities was replaced by another calling. Instead of taking the path solely towards professional self-advancement, many young people of color turned their attention towards fighting institutionalized racism on their campuses and within their own communities. Not only was the study of American history revolutionized, the struggle for ethnic studies became part of a movement to decolonize institutions and urban communities.

International events in the late sixties provided an important backdrop for the rise of Third World activism. Revolutions in the Third World, the rise of Black Power protests led many Third World activists to become more resolved in struggling for liberatory change. There was strong identification with the struggles for independence in Asia, Africa and Latin America; and internal colonialism became an important paradigm used by the activists who saw themselves as part of an oppressed Third World within the U.S. (namely, Asian American, African American, Chicano, Latino American and Native American). This context helped provide the necessary tools for them to look beyond their single ethnicity and see themselves as Asian Americans, African Americans, Native Americans and Chicanos who were part of the Third World.

The vehicle through which these activities took place were the Third World Liberation Front (TWLF) organizations that led the strikes for Ethnic Studies programs at SFS and UCB. The TWLF at SFS included: Black Students Union (BSU), Latin American Students Organization (LASO), the Mexican American Student Confederation (MASC), the Intercollegiate Chinese for Social Action (ICSA), the Philippine Americans for Collegiate Endeavor (PACE); and the Asian American Political Alliance (AAPA). The TWLF at UCB included: Afro-American Student Union (AASU), Asian American Political Alliance (AAPA), Mexican American Student Confederation (MASC) and Native American Student Union (NASU). The SFS TWLF strike began on November 6, 1968 and the UCB TWLF strike followed seventy-seven days later on January 22, 1969. Student activists from both campuses engaged in inter-campus communications as early as Spring Quarter of 1968.

*Introduction*

## How the Demands Came About at SF State and UC Berkeley

Student demands were similar on both sides of the San Francisco Bay. They demanded educational relevance that would meet the needs of their respective communities. This was to be done through the establishment of ethnic studies programs that would include Asian American, African American Studies, Chicano Studies and Native American Studies departments. Of particular emphasis was the demand that the course curriculum was to be "community-based," and that students be able to participate in fieldwork programs in their respective communities.

Listed below were the demands from both campuses:

## BSU SFS Demands

1. That all Black Studies courses being taught through various departments be immediately part of the Black Studies Department and that all the instructors in this department receive full-time pay.
2. That Dr. Hare, Chairman of the Black Studies Department, receive a full-professorship and a comparable salary according to his qualifications.
3. That there be a Department of Black Studies which will grant a bachelor's degree in Black Studies; that the Black Studies Department chairman, faculty and staff have the sole power to hire faculty and control and determine the destiny of its department.
4. That all unused slots for Black Students from Fall 1968 under the Special Admissions program be filled in Spring 1969.
5. That all Black students wishing so, be admitted in Fall 1969.
6. That twenty (20) full-time teaching positions be allocated to the Department of Black Studies.
7. That Dr. Helen Bedesem be replaced from the position of Financial Aid Officer and that a Black person be hired to direct it; that Third World people have the power to determine how it will be administered.
8. That no disciplinary action will be administered in any way to any students, workers, teachers, or administrators during and after the strike as a consequence of their participation in the strike.
9. That the California State College Trustees not be allowed to dissolve any Black programs on or off the San Francisco State College campus.
10. That George Murray maintain his teaching position on campus for the 1968-69 academic year.

## TWLF SF State Demands

1. That a School of Ethnic Studies for the ethnic groups involved in the Third World be set up with the students in each particular ethnic organization having the authority and control of the hiring and retention of any faculty member, director, and administrator, as well as the curriculum in a specific area of study.
2. That 50 faculty positions be appropriated to the School of Ethnic Studies, 20 would be for the Black Studies Program.
3. That in the Spring semester, the College fulfill its commitment to the non-white students by admitting those that apply.
4. That in the Fall of 1969, all applications of non-white students be accepted.

That George Murray and any other faculty person chosen by non-white people as their teacher be retained in their position.[1]

## TWLF UCB Demands:

1. That funds be allocated for the implementation of the Third World College.
   a. Department of Asian Studies controlled by Asian people.
   b. Department of Black Studies as proposed by the AASU.
   c. Department of Chicano Studies.
   d. Department of Native American Studies.

2. Third World People in positions and power. Recruitment of more Third World faculty in every department and discipline and proportionate employment of Third World people at all levels from Regents, Chancellors, Vice-Chancellors, faculty, administrative personnel, clerical, custodial, security services personnel, and all other auxiliary positions and contractual vending services throughout the University system.

3. Specific demands for immediate implementation:
   a. Hiring of Third World Financial Counselors (Special Services).
   b. Third World Chancellors in the University system.
   c. Third World people put in the Placement Center as counselors.
   d. Third World Deans in the L and S Departments.
   e. Third World people in the Admissions Office.

---

[1] George Murray was an English Department lecturer who was dismissed for his participation in the Black Panther Party. SF State Strike Committee, *On Strike: Shut It Down*. 1968. P. 3.

4. Specific demands for immediate implementation:
   a. Admission, financial aid and academic assistance to any Third World student with potential to learn and contribute as assessed by Third World people.
   b. 30 Work Study positions for the Chinatown and Manilatown projects, and 10 EOP counselors, including full-time Asian Coordinator.
   c. Expansion of Work Study program jobs to the AASU East campus Berkeley High School Project, to include at least 30 positions.
   d. That the Center for Chicano Studies be given permanent status with funds to implement its programs.

5. Third World Control over Third World Programs. That every University program financed federally or otherwise that involves the Third World communities (Chicano, Black, Asian) must have Third World people in control at the decision-making level from funding to program implementation.

That no disciplinary action will be administered in any way to any student, workers, teachers, or administrators during and after the strike as a consequence of their participation in the strike.[2]

The students sought complete program autonomy and Third World peoples in positions of power in all decision-making. This included decisions in curriculum, admissions, promotions, research and hiring. In their Third World College Proposal, the UCB TWLF argued that the primary reason for all this was to produce students with the knowledge, expertise, understanding, commitment and desire to identify and present solutions to problems in their respective communities. To SFS and UCB strikers, this could only be done with the establishment of an autonomous school of ethnic studies at SFS, and an autonomous College of Third World Studies at UCB that would have complete control over course curriculum, admissions and hiring.

It would be an understatement to say that the demand for establishment of Ethnic or Third World Studies was opposed by college and university administrators and state government. They were unwilling to accede to the idea of community-based programs that involve students in the decision-making process. Governor Ronald Reagan had taken a hardline position against the student movements in general as a way to rally conservatives behind him for a

---
2   TWLF UCB Strike Demands. *Solidarity Newsletter*. 1969. P. 3.

future presidential nomination bid. He supported repressive measures against the SFS TWLF Strike and eventually declared martial law during the UCB TWLF Strike.

The TWLF proposals were essentially a call to recast the foundations of the education system. It was a challenge to the 1960 Master Plan for Higher Education that called for an "objective" system of testing in the secondary and higher educational system. Students were tracked at an early age by biased intelligence tests. This would determine their fitness for continuing on to either a two-year junior college or a four-year university. In reality, this tracking system proved detrimental to educational advancement in minority communities which lacked qualified teachers and resources. Additionally, standardized testing provisions provided advantage to students from white middle- and upper-class backgrounds and disadvantages for students of colors and poor working class students. The strikers asserted that this was institutionalized racism and Third World minorities were underrepresented in campuses such as SFS and UCB.[3]

## TWLF at San Francisco State

Before their strike began, many Berkeley future TWLF members gained protest experience by attending SF State TWLF strike activities across the bay. The SFS TWLF strike utilized direct mass actions to shut down the campus, with the goal of forcing the administration to come to terms with the strikers. In the aftermath of the assassination of Dr. Martin Luther King and the ensuing urban rebellions across America, TWLF strikers adopted urgent confrontational approaches that disrupted the normal functioning of the campus.

At SF State, the confrontational strategies were responses to unproductive negotiations, broken agreements, and increased use of police on campus. Negotiations had run thin and direct political action became a dominant form of interchange between the College administration and students seeking social justice. Negotiations between the Black Students Union (BSU) and SF State administration had dragged-on unsuccessfully for three years over the establishment of Black Studies curriculum. In November 1967, the BSU took issue with an editorial in the Daily Gator student newspaper that questioned funding for "special programs", including BSU activities. This resulted in the trashing of the newspaper offices and an attack on its editor in which six BSU members were arrested and suspended.[4] In October 1968, Graduate student instructor George

---
3  Strike at Frisco State: the Story Behind It. Research Organizing Cooperative. SF: 1968. PP. 2-8.
4  Orrick Jr., W. H. (1969). *Shut It Down! A College In Crisis*. San Francisco State College. October, 1968--April 1969. S.F., National Commission on the Causes and Prevention of Violence: 22.

Murray, a Black Panther member who taught introductory English classes, was insubstantially quoted in a San Francisco Chronicle article that he had called on Black and Brown students to carry guns to protect themselves from "racist administrators." The reporter was not present at the moment of the alleged statement. Still, the article itself drew the quick ire of the College Trustees and the Mayor's office. This resulted in Murray's October 1968 suspension as a graduate student and instructor for 30 days.[5]

Murray's suspension and the deadlocked negotiations for a Black Studies department led to further polarization between the BSU and the administration. This led to the formation of the TWLF at SFS. The TWLF was a coalition comprised of campus colored minority student organizations that worked in solidarity with the BSU. These organizations included the following: Latin American Students Organization (LASO), Mexican-American Student Confederation (MASC), Intercollegiate Chinese for Social Action (ICSA), Philippine American Collegiate Endeavor (PACE); and Asian American Political Alliance (AAPA). Although the BSU played the impetus role in the formation of the TWLF, its structure allowed for equality in group representation and decision-making. A 12-member central committee was comprised of two delegates from each organization. If there was disagreement, TWLF member groups were allowed the freedom not to participate in TWLF activities.[6]

## Conditions Ripe for Protests at UC Berkeley

Conditions on the campuses were ripe for organized protests. A 1966 race and ethnic survey conducted on the UC Berkeley campus showed a poor track record of minority enrollment. Combined Black, Chicano and Native American student enrollment was 1.5% of the entire student body. From a total UC Berkeley student population of 26,000, only 226 were African American (1.02%), 76 were Chicano (.36%), and 61 were Native American (.28%). By comparison, Black, Chicano and Native Americans comprised approximately 19% of the entire state of California population. Statistics in 1970 showed a 4.7% increase in these three groups which totaled 6.2%. Released numbers included: 1,020 African Americans (3.9%), 381 Chicano (1.4%), 166 Latino (0.6%), 89 Native Americans (0.3%), 2,543 Asian Americans (9.7%) and 15,813 white (60.1%).[7] Minority faculty appointments remained sparse. As

---

5 Ibid. 34-35.
6 Ibid. 100-101. The egalitarian-decision making aspects of the TWLF at S.F. State were forwarded to TWLF-Berkeley during the formative stages of the Berkeley organization. TWLF representative Richard Aoki emphasized this point in a 1995 Ethnic Studies 41AC panel talk at UC Berkeley. This was a popular class on social movements taught by Dr. Carlos Munoz Jr.
7 The earlier figures were from an unpublished source by Matthew Dennis. It was an essay in the

late as 1980, only 1.8% of the faculty was African American. There were only two African American women on a tenured or tenured-track status.

Although Asian Americans fared a little better at around 10% of the campus student population, the figures were challenged as misleading. Before the strike, a report sponsored by the cabinets of the Chinese Students Club and Nisei Students Club acknowledged that Asian Americans appeared overly represented. Out of a campus total of 27,000 students; 2,000 were Asian American who comprised less than 3.5% of the state population (671,000 Asian Americans out of 19,171,000 for the entire statewide population). Both clubs, however, pointed out four misrepresentations of these numbers. Firstly, most of the students were from upper- and middle-class families, while access to higher education was still limited for those from poor urban and rural areas. Secondly, the Filipino American student population remained barely represented. Thirdly, although Asian Studies existed, its focus was in international studies. Fourthly, the hiring of Asians in faculty and administrative positions remained in the lower spectrum of the employment scale. Asian Americans were not present in executive positions.[8]

## Formation of TWLF at UCB

TWLF UCB emerged in a similar pattern as TWLF SFS with African American students initiating the demands and approaching the other Third World groups for reinforcements. Each of the Third World groups had taken the route of approaching the university separately, with separate responses from the administration. Lack of progress for several of the groups negotiating their own minority-based studies programs convinced activists to move toward forming a TWLF coalition. In their view, Third World solidarity was not an ideal but a necessary alliance which developed in-process.[9]

Previously, the Afro-American Student Union (AASU) had conducted nine months of negotiations with the university administration for the establishment of African American Studies. The African American Studies proposal was first submitted to the Chancellor in April 1968. In November, AASU representatives

---

Free Speech Movement Book titled, *The Third World Liberation Front Strike of 1969*. The 19% figure for African American, Chicano and Native American California population percentages are found in 1970 census materials in State of California Department of Finance archives. See website at: dof.ca.gov/html/demograp/race7090.xls. Note here that there was no Chicano census category but Hispanic which combined majority Chicano population with Latinos. The 1970 student demographic materials are from UC Berkeley archives. See: Office of Student Research, UC Berkeley (1970). Enrollments from Fall 1970 to Fall 1985. 2001.

8   NSC and CSC Report. (1968). Fact Sheet by Nisei Students Club and Chinese Students Club of UC Berkeley. Berkeley. Unpublished.
9   *Strike 1969*. (1969) Berkeley Third World Liberation Front. Unpublished.

were asked by the Chancellor to revise the proposal three times. It was then referred to the College of Letters and Science (L&S) for review. L&S then referred the proposal to the Executive Committee of the college, which in turn met and revised the proposal with numerous deletions. The deletions affected important areas of the program's community orientation, fieldwork and student participation in implementation.[10]

By December, African American students and professors were excluded from all meetings and decision-making positions. AASU members and Andrew Billingsley (an African American professor whose position was Assistant to the Chancellor for establishment of Black Studies) were barred from the Executive Committee meeting when these deletions were made. The university administration answered the original twenty-two-page proposal submitted by students and professors was answered with a one-page rejection.[11]

On January 15, 1969, a watered-down Black Studies proposal was finally approved by the College of L&S, but was rejected soundly by the AASU. It was seen as an affront to the principle of self-determination that represented a continuation of the white elite's policy dictating the needs of racial minorities. According to AASU spokesperson Don Davis, "We submitted a program which was well conceived, airtight, and free from any basic flaws. We're not interested in anything less than what we proposed. We've made that clear again and again. No matter what the proposal (L&S version) said, it was wrong because we did not have power to determine our own destinies."[12]

Meanwhile, the Mexican American Students Confederation (MASC) had been undergoing similar experiences. MASC had been involved in a table grape boycott in support of a statewide United Farmworkers Union (UFW) strike. Involving thousands of Mexican and Filipino migrant farmworkers, the strike was one of the largest organizing drives in the Central Valley area of California. At the UC Berkeley campus, strike support work meant the boycott of table grapes and the demand that UC campuses stop all purchases. The campus boycott movement involved a five-month dispute between the university and the Chicano student activists.[13]

---

10  Ibid.
11  Ibid.
12  AASU disagreed on two points which were essentially over control of the department by African American faculty and students; and control over the admission of freshman students into the program. L&S did not want to allow these two points to transpire. Dennis, M. (1995) "Unpublished Report," Ethnic Studies 41 Course Reader, UC Berkeley. Also, see: Duscha, Steve. (January 20, 1969) "Third World Votes—Strike Wednesday." Berkeley. Daily Californian.
13  Strike 1969. (1969) Berkeley Third World Liberation Front. Unpublished.

By August 1968, MASC had reached an agreement with the lower-level University Housing and Food Services officials to remove table grapes from dormitories and the campus food facilities. Both Vice Chancellor Campbell and Business Manager Scott Wilson of Housing and Food Services gave verbal approval for the immediate removal of the table grapes.[14]

On October 1, anti-UFW elements in the state government, including Governor Ronald Reagan and Agricultural Secretary Earl Coke and Superintendent of Public Instruction Max Rafferty, issued strong statements of condemnation of the UFW strike. Shortly thereafter, on October 11th, UC President Hitch issued a statement of neutrality on the UFW strike. He directed purchasing departments (of all nine campuses) not to refuse purchase of any food as a policy decision. This situation set the stage for a half hour meeting on October 14th between MASC representatives and President Hitch. After thirty minutes of deadlocked discussion, President Hitch left the meeting. Eleven MASC representatives were then arrested for unlawful assembly and trespassing.[15]

Three days later, October 17th, President Hitch partially agreed to the establishment of a Center for Mexican American Studies and the appointment of a Chicano Assistant to the President. By Fall, one course in Chicano history was taught at UC Berkeley, while the Center actively recruited Chicanos around the state. Hitch had also given another verbal agreement to remove table grapes from the UC system.[16]

MASC representatives considered these gains important for building towards something larger. Still, the gains were miniscule. The small budget of the Center amounted to $25,000 for the entire program. Final decision-making power, like in the African American Studies program, still rested with a small white elite. MASC representative Manuel Delgado wrote, "The University gave them (Chicanos), as a result of long negotiations and of the arrested eleven Chicanos, an assistant to the President whose contract stipulates that he can do no more than suggest."[17]

In Fall 1968, AAPA had begun negotiations with the university for the establishment of an Asian American Studies curriculum. AAPA meetings were called inviting interested Asian American students to hear and discuss the need for Asian American Studies. The end result was the launch of an experimental

---

14  Ibid.
15  Ibid.
16  Delgado, M. (1999). Presentation at conference titled: The Third World Strike: Historical Lessons. Crossing Over: A Strategy Session and 30 Year Commemoration of the UC Berkeley Third World Strike, Berkeley, Non-Published.
17  Delgado, M. (1969). *TWLF Strike Status*. Berkeley. Unpublished.

course, Asian Studies 100X, during the Winter Quarter of 1969. It was taught under the sponsorship of Professor Franz Schurman from the History Department and Professor Paul Takagi from the Criminology Department. Four graduate students, Bing Thom, Ling-chi Wang, Richard Aoki, and Wai-Kit Quan, all of whom were AAPA members, conducted the actual teaching of these courses, which had an overflowed attendance of four hundred students.

The course title, "The Asian Experience in America," was envisioned to be the genesis for a larger Asian American studies program. The syllabus covered the historical backgrounds of colonialism in China, Japan, Philippines and Korea; Asian American history with specific topics on Asian American labor history; current analysis of modern China and the Vietnam War; and present day Asian American community issues.[18]

The need for a student strike demanding a Third World College at UC Berkeley was raised in follow-up meetings. AAPA members had been approached by the AASU and MASC, whose own negotiations for Black and Chicano Studies programs reached impasse with the administration. AAPA came to the conclusion that the Black and Chicano student experiences with the university bureaucracy would mean that negotiations for Asian American studies could be equally difficult. Discussions then moved towards the mechanics of how to organize a student strike.[19]

Steve Wong, a student who attended the planning meetings, enrolled in AS 100X and later participated in the strike stated, "I took that class because of the influence of the civil rights movement and anti-war movement. It was a natural progression. By then, I felt there shouldn't be so many national boundaries between people. The Asian concept, I felt was much broader than each to his own ethnic group idea. I saw myself as a world citizen. Taking a course like Asian Studies 100X was the way to do it."[20]

Wong had already been active in the San Francisco Chinatown YWCA tutorial project. Growing up with modest means in Sacramento, he viewed tutoring as an important component of social activism to effect positive change. He also believed that political action such as striking for a Third World college was additionally needed to change the political balance of power.[21]

---

18   Fong, B. (2001). Interview With Bryant Fong.
19   Ibid.
20   Wong, Steve. (2001). Interview With Steve Wong. S.F.
21   Ibid.

## Third World Solidarity Emerges

During UCB fall quarter 1968, AASU approached the Asian American and Chicano organizations about forming a TWLF with common demands for a Third World College. Responses varied depending on the progress of each group's own negotiations with the university. MASC representatives had fundamental questions over the issue of equal representation and power. There was also the issue of MASC having recently won a minor victory in the establishment of the Center for Mexican American Studies. According to Manuel Delgado, "We understood that there was a larger struggle for freedom, privilege and respect for Third World people that we had to be a part of. We could not let our specific gains divide us (Third World people)."[22]

Native American Students Union (NASU), the fourth organization to become part of the TWLF, was the smallest group with about five members. NASU's was still in its formative stages and was attempting to locate the few Native Americans present at the UC Berkeley campus. It was not until the beginning of January 1969 that NASU became formally a part of the TWLF. Most of its members were subjects of a governmental relocation program to forcibly assimilate Indians into the mainstream America.[23]

Solidarity among the Third World groups was a new phenomenon influenced by many factors including ideas about internationalism from anti-colonial movements in Asia, Africa and Latin America; as well as the Black Panther Party platform calling for multiracial unity. Additionally, the SF State TWLF strike was influential in implementing Third World unity on US college campuses. Student grievances combined with dismissive responses from college administrators eventually led to political protest and organization.

At Berkeley, white students, individuals and organizations, met separately in TWLF Support Committee meetings. The Support Committee held its own weekly meetings for the purposes of soliciting support and informing the broader student population about the issues of the strike. In many respects, these meetings became the main forum for carrying out policies of the TWLF. Although decision-making powers were subordinated to the TWLF central committee, the general Support Committee meetings encompassed debate over how to conduct strike support. These meetings were attended by a broad spectrum of the radical left including Students for a Democratic Society (SDS), Independent Socialist Club (ISC), Young Socialist Alliance (YSA), and non-affiliated individuals.

---

22  Delgado, M. (1999). The Third World Strike: Historical Lessons. Crossing Over: A Strategy Session and 30 Year Commemoration of the UC Berkeley Third World Strike, Berkeley, Non-Published.
23  War Jack, L. (Ibid.). Third World Strike: Historical Lessons.

The AASU at UCB, having had earlier experience and frustrations in negotiations, was definitely the catalyst in starting the TWLF. The TWLF Constitution draft was the AASU constitution with AASU crossed-off and TWLF written in. But unlike SFS, where the BSU was a separate leading body that formed coalition with the TWLF; at Berkeley, the TWLF included all four ethnic groups in one unit. With the meeting of the various organizations, the creation of the coalition, the coming together of white ally support, the demands written; the students involved in the TWLF at UCB were as ready as they were going to be. Their political actions would lead to reaction and this would begin an upward advancement that would challenge the university and lead to fundamental institutional change.

## TWLF Responds to Repression with Broader Support

At SFS, beginning on November 6, 1968, strikers combined picketing with entering classrooms to call on other students for support. The SF police Tactical Unit was called onto the campus multiple times. On the seventh day of the strike, the Tactical Unit engaged in a confrontation with 2,000 strikers. The police clubbed students in the confrontation and at one point, drew their weapons. Students and faculty demanded that SFS President Robert Smith close down the campus, which he did. The campus closed indefinitely.

Smith was under enormous pressure to keep the campus open at all costs from conservative Republicans who dominated the Board of Trustees, such as State College system Chancellor Glenn S. Dumke, Superintendent of Public Instruction Max Rafferty and Governor Ronald Reagan. On November 25th, Smith organized a Black Students Union-TWLF approved convocation to discuss the issues of the strike while the Trustees met in Los Angeles to discuss the SFS crisis. The convocation ended abruptly the next day (November 26th) when letters of suspension were received by striking students. Smith submitted a letter of resignation to the Trustees citing inability to resolve issues amidst the various political pressures. Immediately, the Trustees named S.I. Hayakawa as the new president of SFS.[24]

Under Hayakawa, confrontations between strikers and police intensified. On December 2nd, Hayakawa instigated a riot when he personally attempted to force open the campus. With the backing of 650 police, Hayakawa climbed onto the strike sound truck, ripped out its wires, shoved students away, and tossed into the air blue armbands which were being passed out to students who were against the strike. The armbands were emblazoned with the letter

---
[24] SFSC Strike Committee. On Strike! 1968. PP 49-51.

"H" which meant support for Hayakawa. Anti-Hayakawa student students rallied and marched to police occupied classrooms where confrontations occurred between thousands of strikers and police. More confrontational incidents occurred through the month of December 1968. The following January 1969, support built for the TWLF with 300 professors who struck for their own union demands as well as TWLF demands. Other campus unions joined in support including clerical, commons and library workers honored the picket lines. Teamsters Union drivers refused to cross picket lines and deliveries to the campus came to a halt.

## Important Strike Junctures at UC Berkeley

The experience of the SFS TWLF was transferred to Berkeley. Berkeley students were up against a similar institutional structure. Instead of the Board of Trustees, the UC student strikers had to deal with the UC Regents who were appointed by Governor Ronald Reagan and were opposed to the student demands for the Third World College. There was pressure from Governor Ronald Reagan, who felt that the university administration should take a hard line towards the students. Eager to win votes, Reagan took every opportunity to express his opposition towards student protest. At the same time, the university was concerned about a public perception of UC being too repressive towards minority students.[25]

On January 22, the first task at hand for the UCB TWLF was to station informational picket lines in front of various entries to the university. Initial student responses were nondescript and dependent upon the spirited of the chanting and singing on the picket lines. Protestors borrowed chants from the Southern civil rights and Black Power movement with slight variations. Instead of "Black Power," "Third World power" was inserted. Manuel Delgado recalled, "First we chanted, 'say it loud, I'm black and I'm proud... and then we alternated with I'm brown and I'm proud, followed with I'm red and I'm proud, followed with I'm yellow and I'm proud, and I'm white and I'm proud. We even added I'm bourgeoisie and I'm proud. We all laughed."[26]

That night, a fire destroyed Wheeler Auditorium. A shocked TWLF central committee quickly issued a public statement disavowing any connection with the fire. UCB Chancellor Roger Heyns implied that the strike precipitated acts of violence; however, the fire bureau laboratory tests failed to show supporting evidence of arson. Through the duration of the strike, the campus

---
25 Kitchell, M. (1990) Film: *Berkeley in the 60's*. Kitchell Films. Berkeley.
26 Delgado, M. *Third World Strike, Historical Lessons*. Crossing Over Conference Presentation. Berkeley.

administration and the press brought up charges of TWLF-sponsored violence and property damage to discredit the legitimacy of the strikers' demands.[27]

Support from the campus-wide American Federation of Teachers, Local 1570 (Teaching Assistants), occurred incrementally. Initially, Local 1570 called for a work stoppage, between January 22 and January 27, in support of the strike. On January 27, a strike vote was taken, narrowly defeating support for the strike. Later, on February 13, the police completely surrounded an AFT Local 1570 picket line in support of TWLF strike and arrested 36 people. This occurred despite the fact that the line moved and allowed people to pass through. The arrests created further momentum to support the strike. On February 18, AFT Local 1570 voted to strike in support of the TWLF strike and union organizing rights.[28]

On January 30, UCB administration announced that disciplinary action would be taken against "identified students who violated campus regulations." In response, the Associated Students of the University of California (ASUC) Senate, the governing student body, passed a resolution condemning "disruptive and violent tactics" and urged students and faculty to pressure the Administration to implement a department of Afro-American Studies. The resolution also supported the Administration's efforts to consider the possible advantages of instituting a College of Ethnic Studies.

Academic faculty support was inconsistent and became dependent upon the increase in confrontations between police and strikers. On January 27, the overwhelming majority of Third World faculty and administrators signed a public statement giving support to the strike. On February 5, the Academic Senate was reluctant to fully support resolutions favoring the principle of an autonomous College of Ethnic Studies organized by Third World faculty and students. The resolution was tabled until one month later. It was not until March 4 that the Academic Senate endorsed the establishment of an interim Ethnic Studies Department responsible only to Chancellor, with the TWLF allowed to formulate the curriculum.[29]

After entering a short period of informational picketing, the TWLF gave notice that unless demands were met, Sather Gate would be blocked. On February 4, 1969, the escalation of tactics entailed the sealing of Sather Gate Bridge, a major cross-campus thoroughfare, with shoulder-to-shoulder stationary picketers blocking off the bridge.[30]

---
27  *Strike 1969.* (1969) Berkeley Third World Liberation Front. Unpublished.
28  *Strike 1969.* (1969) Berkeley Third World Liberation Front. Unpublished.
29  Ibid.
30  (1969, February 4). Police Again Confront Pickets. <u>Daily Californian</u>. Berkeley: 1

TWLF's intention was to disrupt traffic flow in order to call attention to the demands and principles of the strike. Debates occurred immediately between striking and non-striking students over the issue of freedom of access. There were alternative access routes which suggested the complaints over access were a moot point. Though the TWLF intended the seal-off to be a symbolic political action, police overreaction further polarized the situation. The disruption became further aggravated when the stationary line was attacked by undercover police officers as they attempted to arrest student protestors on the strike line. Forty campus police and Alameda County Sheriff officers entered into a pitched confrontation with demonstrators. The events culminated in fifteen arrests and twenty injuries.[31]

In the face of overwhelming police presence, on February 5th, the TWLF adopted a serpentine formation protest march around campus. Instead of holding ground in the traditional manner of sit-ins, the mobile snake-shaped moving picket line allowed the flexibility of mobility in the face of police attack and enabled outreach to students who began to sympathize with their fellow students. The disruptive effect was no longer contained within the traditional central campus rallying area but became more dispersed and difficult to contain.[32]

Even during the peaceful informational picket period of the strike, the issue of police misconduct was a heated issue. This was highlighted in the January 29th arrest and the beating of AASU/TWLF member Cordell Abercrombie. He had been a visible strike captain on the picket line. As a strike captain and chant leader with the sound bullhorn, he had played a vocal role in maintaining strike line organization. According to TWLF spokesman Fernando Garcia, Abercrombie was arrested in the evening as he was walking across campus. Garcia stated that Abercrombie was neither charged nor told of his constitutional rights when taken into custody. He was allegedly held and beaten in the Sproul Administration by six police officers.[33]

On February 13th, police moved to break up a moving picket line of 1,000 strikers on Sproul Plaza. Police attempted to clear picketers walking on the administration steps when several TWLF leaders persisted in picketing on the steps. Arrests were made which resulted in physical confrontation between police and protestors. Six university employees reported they witnessed

---
31  Ibid.
32  Bartl, J. (1969, February 5). Strike Violence Grows, Police Invade Campus. Daily Californian. Berkeley: 1.
33  According to a statement by the TWLF, on February 13, 1969, statements signed by 12 university employees and independently by others recounted indiscriminate, severe beatings by police in the basement of Sproul Hall. *Strike 1969*. (1969) Berkeley, Third World Liberation Front. Unpublished.

plainclothes Alameda County Sheriffs beat arrested demonstrators in detention. The witnesses wrote an open letter to the Daily Californian to expose the violence.[34]

A February 13th editorial in the Daily Californian called upon students to oppose the police terror and support the demands of the TWLF. It also pointed out that the teaching assistants' union, on strike because of police terror, may be fired for striking. The editorial asserted, "The blood-stained beasts stalk the campus. The police have suspended the constitution and are making arrests at will, and without provocation. They then proceed to rarified forms of torture."[35]

Law enforcement had used the strategy of isolating the leadership from the rank-and-file. Speakers at rallies and strike captains would be identified in police or media photographs. They would become targeted for ensuing arrests. Sometimes this was comical when it came to Asian Americans. Because they "all looked alike," one Asian American would be arrested because he looked like another Asian American who had made a public statement to the media.[36]

## Balance Between Directions, Actions and Negotiations

Negotiations between the TWLF representatives and the Chancellor's office mirrored the intensity of protest activity on the strike lines. Sometimes, strike activities caused cancellation of negotiation sessions. One session was cancelled when a confrontation was taking place within window eyesight of both the TWLF negotiation team and Chancellor Roger Heyns. The daily strike activities and mounting support resolutions by professors, teaching assistants and community organizations comprised an important backdrop to the negotiations. Student response to campus repression rallied more widespread support. Both students and professors, who at first marginally supported the strike, became drawn in because of the martial law-like atmosphere of the campus that limited them from doing campus business as usual.

The following events encapsulated the different swings between strike activities and institutional response:

*February 4: UCB. Twenty arrested and twenty were injured when plainclothes officers attempted to arrest strikers. Police declared strike support activity in Sproul Plaza an "illegal assembly" and ordered people to disperse.*

---

34  Dillion, R. Sproul Beatings Reported. (1969, February 19) Daily Californian. Berkeley.
35  Editorial: The Horror. Daily Californian. Berkeley. (1969, February 13) Daily Californian.
36  Aoki, R. (2001). Interview with Richard Aoki.

*February 5: UCB. Administration canceled noon rallies because of the possibility of violence--a clear case of prior restraint. Governor Ronald Reagan declared a "state of extreme emergency" on the campus and surrounding areas to enable more California Highway Patrol to enter campus.*

*February 8: UCB. Chancellor's Office and TWLF Progress Committee reached a tentative agreement on creating an implementing committee (2 students and 2 faculty from each group), but the agreement was then repudiated. Chancellor claimed that TWLF repudiated the agreement; TWLF faculty claimed that Heyns said "key faculty" would not approve it.*

*February 10 UCB. Subcommittee of Dean Knight's Committee on Ethnic Studies (headed by East Asian Studies Professor George DeVos) recommended that Third World faculty draw up the proposals for the creation of a College of Third World Studies. TWLF criticized the report for excluding students and for forwarding the proposals to regular administrative and faculty channels, where TW faculty would be only ex-officio (non-voting) members.*

*February 19. UCB. Negotiations between TWLF and Chancellor Roger Heyns broke down on the powers of the implementing committee. Chancellor claimed that the TWLF demand would "compromise the integrity of campus academic review procedures" and if the TWLF would not accept his proposal, "we will, of course, seek other ways and other students and faculty members who are willing."*

*February 26, Heyns broke off negotiations because of "violence" of the strikers. This occurred at the time of the brutal arrest of MASC member Manuel Delgado. After he was arrested, Ysidro Macias was clubbed on the back of his head and arrested. He was unconscious for several hours. This incident resulted in student confrontation with police, who used clubs and teargas*

*February 27: UCB. First use of National Guard on campus. Police used teargas to drive students off campus. This represented intense pressure from Governor Reagan's office to intervene in campus negotiations.*[37]

By the end of February, there was apprehension among AAPA members that the strike may have been getting out of hand. Clashes with police were becoming intense, with large police presence and the introduction of CS teargas dropped by helicopter. By February 22nd, the university announced that 127 individuals had been arrested. Arrested students were immediately placed on

---

[37] *Strike 1969*. (1969) Berkeley. Third World Liberation Front. Unpublished. According to the Berkeley Daily Gazette, on February 20th, over 1,000 National Guard were on standby at the Berkeley Marina and in Alameda. How Long Will the Guard Remain? (1969, February 22) Berkeley Daily Gazette. Berkeley: 1.

interim suspension and barred from strike participation. There was fear that the eventual declaration of martial law by Governor Reagan would make negotiations for Third World College demands exceedingly difficult. At a press conference, the Governor argued for the establishment of martial law. He stated that the police had run out of tear gas and that the National Guard would be present to replenish the depleted supply and to provide support to law enforcement.[38]

On the evening of Thursday February 20th, an emergency AAPA meeting was conducted to discuss the question of how to handle the immense confrontations between strikers and the police. There was debate late into the night about the intensification of the conflict. Positions were polarized between "soft-liners" and the "hardliners." The soft-liners felt that the violence had gotten out of hand. The strike was being taken over by "crazy white radicals," and was no longer controlled by Third World people. They feared that the ongoing negotiation process between the TWLF and the chancellor's office would be replaced by military martial law. The hardliners felt that there was the need to intensify the protests and that the only basis for negotiations was the mass pressure on strike lines. One hardliner argued that it was not just a question of fighting for a Third World College but one of defeating a power structure that was responsible for the slaughter in Vietnam.[39]

The resulting vote was twenty to "cool it," and seven to continue on the same militant path. Upon taking a majority vote, the other TWLF leadership members were contacted, and on the following day, TWLF monitors went among the crowds of students and high school youth and gave the directive that no violence should occur. Three thousand strikers and protestors rallied outside the February 22nd Regents meeting attended by Governor Reagan, in one of the largest support rallies held. It was also one of the more peaceful ones, with strike leadership calling for calmness. According to one local newspaper, strike leaders and monitors went into the crowds asking them to "be cool, no rock-throwing and don't give Reagan an excuse to call out the guard."[40]

According to the *Berkeley Daily Gazette*, this was also the largest show of organized law enforcement presence in Berkeley history. Over twenty law enforcement agencies comprised a police mutual aid force of six hundred police and highway patrol officers. Over three hundred riot police were in visible view of the protest, and three hundred more were stationed in nearby parking garages. Fifty armed National Guardsmen were present with equipment

---

38  Cant, G. (Ibid.). Police Mass on Campus
39  Li, A (2001) Interview with Arnold Li. S.F.
40  Cant, G. (1969, February 22). Police Mass On Campus. Berkeley Daily Gazette. Berkeley: 1.

vehicles and an Army helicopter. One thousand more National Guard soldiers were encamped on a military facility in nearby Alameda.[41]

The cooling-off tactic did prove the "sincerity" of the TWLF to negotiate for a settlement. At the same time, there was the feeling among many strikers that little would be resolved by cooling off and that what was needed was more strike action. The Regents voted to suspend students when there was "reasonable cause to believe" they had violated campus rules. Negotiations with the Chancellor continued but remained inconclusive. As more violence and arrests continued--including the arrest of strike leaders and the use of tear gas—the Chancellor broke off meetings. Finally, on February 27, 1969, Governor Reagan acted with the official order to send National Guard into the UC Berkeley campus—effectively, making it an armed camp.[42]

## Ethnic Studies Established

On March 4, the Academic Senate voted 550 to 4 in support of an interim Ethnic Studies Department responsible only to the Chancellor. The Senate allowed for Third World student participation in the formulation of course curriculum, with a promise that its structure would be "of sufficient flexibility to permit evolution into a college." The Chancellor announced that the department would "immediately offer four-year programs leading to a B.A. degree in history, culture, and contemporary experience of ethnic minority groups, especially Black Americans, Mexican Americans, Asian Americans, and Native Americans." Each of the four groups would comprise a division within the interim Ethnic Studies department.[43]

After final approval UC system-wide President Hitch announced the Ethnic Studies Department was scheduled to begin instruction in Fall Quarter 1969. In response, the TWLF suspended strike activities. A TWLF strike moratorium was declared with the stipulation that the strike could be reactivated at any moment if negotiations over the Third World College demands reached impasse.[44] The strike moratorium did not lead to a final settlement, only a stalemate that continued for many decades.

Meanwhile, at S.F. State, President Hayakawa stated publicly that granting Ethnic Studies demands was the only alternative to move past three semesters of student strife. He acknowledged that Third World student frustrations stemmed from being excluded from academic opportunities. At the same time,

---

41  Ibid.
42  Wang, L.L. (1997). Chronology of Ethnic Studies at U.C. Berkeley. Berkeley. Unpublished.
43  Ibid.
44  Strike 1969. (1969) Berkeley. Third World Liberation Front. Unpublished.

Hayakawa drew a distinction between students who participated because they wanted inclusion and other students who participated because of new left ideologies. He supported the former but asserted that there was nothing he could do for the latter.[45]

At SFS, the first School of Ethnic Studies in the nation was established which was able to confer degrees in Ethnic Studies, American Indian Studies, Asian American Studies, Black Studies and La Raza Studies. Now called the College of Ethnic Studies, it remains today the only college of its kind in the nation. The college has its own dean and separate department chairs. Instructors and majors are required to participate in community engagement. In 2016, budget cuts at SFS amounting to $245,000 threatened the programs and four ethnic studies departments. In response, students went on a ten-day hunger strike to save the college. The protest received wide support and resulted in rescinding the cuts and financial commitments that amounted to an additional $482,000, four work-study programs, funding to develop Pacific Islander Studies, and the formation of a task force consisting of students, faculty, staff and administrators to continue the dialogue.[46] UC Berkeley students, mostly graduate students, and a few instructors had also attended SF State rallies.

## UC Berkeley Ethnic Studies Shorthanded From Start

UC Berkeley, on the other hand, received smaller budget allocations for an interim Department of Ethnic Studies with programs in Asian American, African American, Chicano and Native American Studies. Each of the programs also conferred Bachelor of Arts degrees. In 1969, there were valid concerns among Berkeley TWLF strikers over how far an interim Ethnic Studies Department could develop and whether future generations of students would be able to continue pressing the university towards the goal of a Third World College. The interim state of the department eventually became hamstrung by future administration program cuts and reorganizations, making it difficult for future generations to develop the interim department into a college.

While in the beginning, Ethnic Studies was controlled by students, eventually, the University increased pressures to wrest away student power. In 1974, the Collins Committee, a review board under the academic senate, recommended the removal of community engagement components. For Asian Studies, as what Asian American Studies was called then, this meant the cutting off of funding for its community components that included: support for the Asian

---

[45] Orrick Jr., W. H. (1969). *Shut It Down! A College In Crisis. San Francisco State College.* October, 1968--April 1969. S.F., National Commission on the Causes and Prevention of Violence: 172.

[46] Herrera, Jack. Stanford University. USA Today. May 22, 2016

Studies Field Office located in San Francisco Manilatown, funding for Field Work Assistant positions that placed students in community projects and organizations in SF and Oakland Chinatowns, SF Manilatown and SF Japantown. Student input and leadership was also removed from decision-making roles in the department in varying degrees.

To weaken demands for the TW College, it was proposed that the different ethnic programs within Ethnic Studies separate into their own departments within the College of Letters and Science (L&S). Small budgets and increased pressure to separate Ethnic Studies programs eventually led to the exit of African American Studies from the Ethnic Studies in 1974 to form its own department within L&S. With three remaining programs (Asian, Chicano and Native American), Ethnic Studies added a Comparative Ethnic Studies Program to compensate for the void caused by the departure of African American Studies. Ethnic Studies continued for twenty years as an interim department under the UC Chancellor's office without any serious strategy for long-term survival.

In 1995, the Department of Ethnic Studies, pressured by the administration, entered L&S as the only alternative for long-term survival. However, entry into L&S did not result in the perceived increased program funding and support. The benign neglect continued. Many Ethnic Studies department classes disappeared, retired professor slots were not replaced, and community studies ceased to exist in any substantial systemized way. In 1999, a crisis situation led students to take political action invoking activist ideals from 30 years earlier. A new twLF was formed by students who organized a sit-in at Barrows Hall and a hunger strike to protest class cuts, to demand that retired faculty slots be replaced, and that additional professors be hired. Both Ethnic Studies and African American Studies faculty supported the student demands and actions. Faculty, students and community representatives participated in outdoor rallies. The students in 1999 were eventually able to save Ethnic Studies for that moment in 1999 as well as to obtain funding for the establishment of the Center for Race & Gender, the Multicultural Community Center and a twLF mural in Barrows Hall.

Other crisis followed and student organizing again took place in 2010 and 2017, with varying degrees of success and support. In 2010, Operation Excellence led to cutbacks, consolidation and layoffs. There was a short student hunger strike. Ethnic studies town hall meetings were organized by graduate students and faculty. The dialogue started well with meetings and "breaking bread" meals and discussions but ended without resolution. In 2017, undergraduate students formed a "1969 twLF Collective" to create more dialogue within Ethnic Studies faculty to voice concerns over teaching pedagogy and direction. The results turned badly with dialogue ceasing to take place and trust between faculty and students at a low point.

The previous occurrence that I write about is not isolated but very much a part of struggles taking place on college campuses across the country. Ethnic Studies today faces challenges from the outside and from within, as noted by Dr. Gary Okhiro, where the fight is not only against white supremacy but also involves an internal battle within the university over what counts as "self-determination."[47] Fortunately, students and sometimes faculty continue to resist neoliberal rationalizations of budget cuts. In 2016, at San Francisco State University (or SFSU), students launched a 10-day hunger strike to protest budget cuts and instructor layoffs in the College of Ethnic Studies.[48] In 2019, at Yale University, thirteen faculty members withdrew their services from the Ethnicity, Race, and Migration Program for lack of university support.[49] If we place such actions in a broader context of defending and expanding Ethnic Studies programs, an interconnection with the 1968–69 Third World Strike is evident.

Unquestionably, the establishment of ethnic studies programs has been one of the chief legacies of the TWLF strikes. Similar programs have grown nationally in over 250 universities, colleges and high schools. Both UC Berkeley and SF State University now provide undergraduate and graduate degree programs in Ethnic Studies. Legislation continues to offer ethnic studies courses in grades 9-12 in California. There is a movement in California to establish K-12 ethnic studies. But while there is growing demand for ethnic studies, class offerings on many college campuses are low which, in turn, discourage program growth.

A most often forgotten legacy of the strikes was the building of solidarity among the different racial and ethnic groups who struggled to change the educational environment. This solidarity was important in community struggles such as the International Hotel anti-eviction movement and Alcatraz Island Indian movement when many former TWLF participants took lessons from the campus struggles to their own communities. Another important legacy can be

---

47 Okihiro, Gary. "The Future of Ethnic Studies: the Field is Under Assault from Without and Within." The Chronicle of Higher Education, July 04, 2010.
48 Herrera, Jack. "10-day hunger strike one-fourth victory for SFSU students." USA Today, May 22, 2016.
49 Wanna, Carly. "Thirteen Professors Withdraw from ER&M Majors in Limbo." Yale Daily News, March 29, 2019.

found in the ethnic studies community-related programs that led to the establishment of important community institutions in the San Francisco Bay Area such as La Clinica De La Raza and Asian Health Services

In 2018-2019, veterans of the 1969 strike and Ethnic Studies activists from 1999 and recent struggles commemorated the TWLF 50th anniversary. They participated in a series of events including teach-ins, intergenerational mixers, breaking bread meals, exhibits, and forums. The events principally focused on addressing concerns that affect the department, including the incompleteness of the demand for the Third World College. Educators, students, and members from communities under attack, such as those currently facing federal draconian anti-immigration policies, as well as organizers struggling to establish ethnic studies in the high schools; participated in discussions. The TWLF 50th anniversary attempted, in many ways, to rebuild trust among students, faculty, staff and community. Moving forward requires recognition that the strength of ethnic studies has always been to rely on student activism rooted in community to ensure continuation of a truly relevant education.

# Chapter One:
# Origins & Background

*Sealing-off Sather Gate by TWLF, UC Berkeley. January 1969. Doug Wachter photo.*

# Bandung: The Third World Project

JANIE CHEN

> *"The Third World was not a place. It was a project. During the seemingly interminable battles against colonialism, the peoples of Africa, Asia, and Latin America dreamed of a new world."*[50]
>
> Vijay Prashad, The Darker Nations: A People's History of the Third World

*Photo from Bandung Indonesia, 1955. Photo: LSE Blogs.*

During the 1955 Bandung Conference in Indonesia, the Third World project was launched. Delegates from 29 "underdeveloped" Asian and African nations, such as Burma, India, Pakistan, and Sudan, gathered to strategize a platform of demands in the face of growing Western imperial forces. Much more than the Cold War conflict happening at the time, what emerged from the Bandung Conference was a set of political declarations echoing the principles of international cooperation, sovereignty, recognition and equality of all races, mutual interests and justice. It was the making of an Afro-Asian solidarity and framework that would soon precede a rich but subterranean tradition of collaborative radical politics and resistance in post-colonial eras. The impacts and legacy of this monumental alliance between Afro-Asian peoples reverberated across time and nations, particularly in 1960s where the Third World Liberation Front (TWLF) was to be ignited in San Francisco and Berkeley, California.

---

50  Vijay Prashad. The Darker Nations: A People's History of the Third World. (New York: New Press, 2007), xv.

The Bandung Conference was initiated by political leaders of China, Indonesia, India, Pakistan, Myanmar, and Sri Lanka to address the economic decentralization of resources and issues of human rights, self-determination and peace. The conference was situated in a history of anti-colonial and anti-imperialist efforts. In its universal declaration, they expressed that "colonialism in all its manifestation is an evil which should speedily be brought to an end."[51] Bandung can be understood as a much larger project, one of collective imagination and political process that inspired a range of social movements. It established a collective "New World Consciousness," a decolonized way of analyzing the conditions of Third World peoples. Though the alliances later disseminated, its spirit became instrumental in the making of Afro-Asian solidarity. Similar to how Afro-Asian nations congregated at the Bandung Conference, an unprecedented coalition of student organizations amassed at the campuses of SFS and UC Berkeley.

Rooted in working class struggle, the TWLF consisted of African American, Chicanx, Latinx, Asian American, and Native American students who adopted and carried the "Bandung spirit" to historically oppressed communities of color in the US. The TWLF embodied similar calls of Third World solidarity, self-determination and an education relevant to their communities and histories. Like Bandung, I situate the TWLF within the long-fought struggle of historically oppressed communities for self-determination.

Understanding the grievances that pushed students to form the TWLF necessitates the understanding of the impact and legacy of slavery, colonialism, the "yellow peril," and genocide of Native Americans that occurred over the course of four centuries. Their demands and visions were therefore intimately tied with colonialism and racism as they confronted basic questions of power and oppression in one area of their lives – education. And their education under the authority of white, out of touch administration in their ivory tower had failed to include what was accurate and relevant to the experiences of minority groups.

Like Bandung, there was also an urgency for greater solidarity between Black and Asian communities. Students of color on the SFS and UCB campuses understood the high drop out and disengagement rates among their peers as a symbolic violence wielded by white supremacy. In identifying a common adversary in their struggle for liberation, the TWLF cultivated a "New World Consciousness" through their mutually shared oppressions. Asian American students recognized their struggle and needs were interdependent upon other

---

51  America and the Postwar World: Remaking International Society, 1945-1956. David Mayer.

people of color. The Black community, particularly the Black Panthers, was a major factor in profoundly impacting large numbers of Asian Americans to begin questioning the legitimacy of American democracy. By pinpointing the juncture between state violence and impoverished communities, the Black activists contributed a language and discourse that placed the Asian American experience in a global context of race and capitalism.

Happening at the same time of the TWLF was the anti-war movement. The late 1960s was one of the most tumultuous eras in post-WW2 history. The changing national and global landscape was characterized by revolutionary struggles influenced by the Civil Rights Movement and the Vietnam War. Martin Luther King Jr. called the war a "symptom of a far deeper malady within the American spirit" because at the same time the US was engaging in clandestine military operations abroad, it was criminalizing Black protest at home. Reminiscent of Third World struggles in the Bandung Era, America had proven itself to be a living contradiction as its rhetoric of protecting democracy abroad was at odds with its reality domestically. Therefore, multi-racial solidarity and collaboration reflected a stance reminiscent of the Bandung Conference, a stance grounded in anti-imperialism and anti-oppression. TWLF strikers during the heyday of the movement echoed Malcolm X's "by any means necessary." Meanwhile, the Student Nonviolent Coordinating Committee (SNCC), led by Stokely Carmichael, chanted "Hell, no, we won't go!" at a UN demonstration. Muhammed Ali refused to be drafted into the army as African Americans joined the forefront of opposition against US involvement in Southeast Asia.

Bandung may not resonate strongly as it did during the late 1960s, but it is important to recognize the powerful influence it had in shaping the TWLF movement. It laid the international political landscape from which the TWLF emerged and its spirit carried into future strikes for Third World education. As shown through the 1999 and late 2000 resurgences, the movement for Third World liberation is intergenerational and has lasting impacts on future political mobilizations.

*TWLF strike activities, UC Berkeley. January February 1969. Doug Wachter photo.*

# Dr. Carlos Munoz Jr: An Inspiration For All of Us

*PABLO GONZALEZ*

Dr. Carlos Munoz faced 66 years in prison for his participation in organizing high school walkout protests against racism, poor education in the East Los Angeles schools. During the first week of March 1968, over 22,000 students from Garfield, Lincoln, Wilson, Roosevelt, Belmont, Venice and Jefferson High School walked out in what was called the East LA Blowouts. (Zinn Education Project)

*East Los Angeles Chicano Blowouts, 1968. Chicano Student Newspaper photo.*

Audacity! The word still echoes when I think about what lured me towards ethnic studies at UC Berkeley in the mid-1990s. With furor and passion, it was repeated often in my lower division course on ethnic social movements to describe the violence of the state during the tumultuous 1960s struggles. I wanted to speak with such passion. I wanted to indict power similarly. It spoke to the "ya basta!" to the growth of anti-immigrant legislation, to the lack of funding for ethnic studies, to the attacks on the gains of the sixties. Spoken by an icon of the sixties, Dr. Carlos Munoz Jr. inspired thousands of students and people through his years of activism and teaching.

The following interview with Dr. Carlos Munoz Jr., professor emeritus of Ethnic Studies, is a small piece of an amazing life dedicated to social justice. The interview reinforces what many ethnic studies scholars studying the 1960s have suggested, that the politicization of Mexican Americans, especially veterans, begins with war. Munoz Jr. describes how war was the key marker for understanding and analyzing imperialism and conceptualizing what we now term "Third World" politics. Having received the opportunity to attend college in Los Angeles, Munoz Jr. makes a crucial connection between US imperialism and racialized non-white groups in the United States. Those being sent to Korea or Vietnam were not only poor but Black and Brown. Audacity took on its first meaning for Munoz Jr. It meant questioning years of institutional Americanization of Mexican Americans. After being honorably discharged from the military, Munoz Jr. received a GI Bill to attend college. It is in the university where he was exposed to the writings of Martiniquean revolutionary, Frantz Fanon and Mexican anthropologist, Pablo Gonzalez Casanova. While Fanon described the colonizer/colonized condition, Gonzalez Casanova theorized what Munoz Jr. would further as a concept, the "internal colony" model.

For Munoz Jr., the "internal colony" model in the United States resembled the long history of dispossession, racism, and oppression faced by racialized groups like Mexican Americans in the United States. He would connect the "internal colony" model to the histories of Mexicans, Blacks, and Asians in the US and to the plight of students of color in universities. As student president for one of the most important Chicano student organizations of the time, United Mexican American Students or UMAS, Munoz Jr. sought to follow his growing Third World politicization by building coalitions with Black students at Cal State Los Angeles in 1967. Demanding Black Studies and Mexican American Studies, Mexican Americans and Black students would help create some of the first programs dedicated to Black and Mexican Americans in the United States. Munoz Jr., now a graduate student would play a critical role in building cross-racial coalitions, teaching us the value of such alliances inside and outside of the classroom.

In 1968, as the chair of the first Mexican American Studies program in the nation at Cal State LA, looked to bridging the activism of the university to the growing militancy of high school students in East Los Angeles. While still a graduate student, Munoz Jr. believed that Mexican American Studies should have a greater connection between the university and the community. Munoz Jr. felt that internal colonization began in the schools and he along with other college students looked to high school mobilization as a source of inspiration and activism. This key moment in 1968 lead to the monumental East LA blowouts of March 1968, where thousands of students walked out of classrooms to protest the continued inequality in the schools. His support of students put him in the crosshairs of FBI and local police surveillance. It eventually led to his arrest and the arrest of twelve others on charges of conspiracy to disrupt the school system. The famous "thirteen" Chicanos faced sixty-six years in prison if convicted.

After the charges were dropped, Munoz Jr. continued working on his PhD and the concept of "internal colonialism." He would eventually leave Los Angeles to take a position at UC Berkeley as one of the first Chicano Studies and Ethnic Studies professors who received positions after the success of the Third World Liberation Front strike in 1969. Decades later, Dr. Carlos Munoz Jr. continues to show what a true comrade and colleague, dedicated to liberation and social justice, represents. His "audacity" that gave many of us the inspiration and energy to articulate our own cry still rings true throughout the halls of East Los Angeles high schools and places like Sproul Hall at the most prestigious of universities.

(Pablo Gonzalez is a lecturer in the Chicano Studies Program and Ethnic Studies Department, UC Berkeley.)

## High School Blowouts—East Los Angeles

*Lincoln High School walkout against education inequality in East Los Angeles, 1968. Chicano Student News Photo.*

## High School Walkouts—Oakland

*Oakland High students protest police murder of Panther Bobby Hutton. 1968. Nikki Arai photo.*

# What Happened After I Left the Military

*CARLOS MUNOZ JR*

*Excerpts from an interview with UCB Ethnic Studies Professor Emeritus Carlos Munoz who came to UC Berkeley after the strike to establish the Third World College. Interview by Harvey Dong (2018).*

 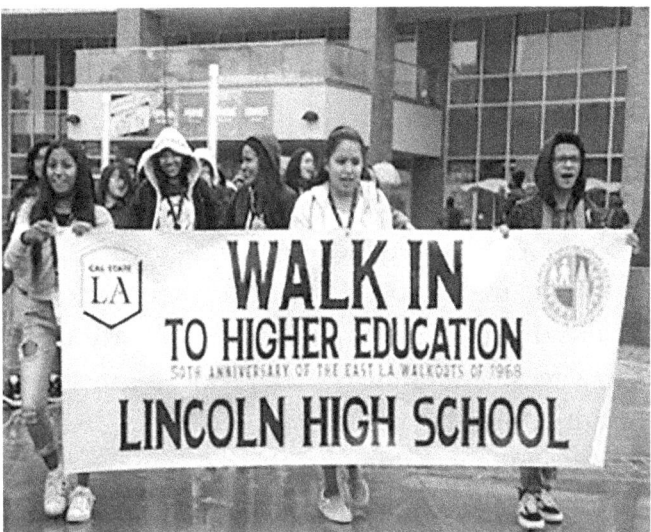

Left: Dr. Carlos Munoz, Jr. Right: Cal State LA commemorates 50th Anniversary of walkout at Lincoln High School. Wave News

So when I was able to leave the military service, I left with an honorable discharge in 1962. I went back home to begin planning for college and of course, a job first, which I couldn't find for a long time. I started going to community college at night. I worked in the day from 8am to 5pm and afterwards, I went to L.A. City College at night. By then, the war had become very visible. More casualties, more troops. It was official… there was a war. No more secret cover. Those of us who were not in Vietnam were on other battleground stations like South Korea where there was the possibility of combat. When the first combat veterans started coming back to organize against the war, I joined them and became a member of the Vietnam Veterans Against the War. I was able to get the GI bill along with the other Vietnam combat veterans. I joined them in the movement against the war and became an activist.

1965 was my first demonstration. President Johnson was in town in L.A. and I was one of the thousands among the crowd. It was one of the first major demonstrations against the war. And man, you know, I was really into it. I said we've gotta stop the goddamn war. I started thinking along those lines that the war was an imperialist action. We were not a democracy. We were an imperialist empire. I became very well versed in redefining what we call the 'Third World.' European empires were colonizing Africa, South America and Asia. So, I began looking at that more critically and reading more about it. In my college courses, I came across Frantz Fanon. I also came across a Mexican sociologist with the name of Castaneda who wrote about Mexico. And I began looking at the indigenous as colonized, internally colonized people in Mexico.

Wow, that really turned me on. I had begun to see the connections here in the U.S. I began to look at those of us who were Mexican, Black, Asian, and other groups here who were oppressed as internal colonies of the U.S. empire. I wasn't quite articulating it in that way then, but my mind was set there. No one had yet come up with any books or writings on it.

When the GI bill kicked in, I began getting active on campus. I was able to stop working full-time and instead get a part-time campus job. I became very involved with campus politics at Cal State Los Angeles in 1967. In 1968, I became president of the United Mexican American Student (UMAS) coalition and began connecting with the leadership in the Black Student Union (BSU). I started working with them to blend together a black-brown coalition that would ignite some action on behalf of the Black and brown kids on campus.

One of our first actions was to invite Muhammed Ali to speak against the war on our campus. As you know, he was under indictment because he had refused to serve in Vietnam. That was an experience. So anyways, I'm walking with Muhammed Ali on one side and Bob Smith on the other. I look up to this buy guy, beautiful guy. I said, "Hey Muhammed, you should be my bodyguard. What am I going to do if someone attacked you? I couldn't do shit about that but if I get attached, you could help."

We activists got a house. We called it the Black and Brown House where the BSU and UMAS would take turns having meetings. We began to have a rapport, a comradeship. The other action after that was to demand a Black Studies department and Mexican American Studies department. I led the charge on that. We infiltrated the administration, basically. We had people who were working part-time in the administration. I called them our CIA, Chicano Intelligence Agency. We got the approval for the programs in 1968 — first time in any part of the country at that time. We became the first department of Chicano Studies and called it Mexican American Studies at the time. Chicano didn't get its coinage until the following year. Following that achievement, we also got Black Studies.

At the time, I was a young father of two, working on my masters, and thinking about a PhD. I didn't have time, but I felt compelled to serve as the UMAS chair. I became a first-year graduate student and the first chair in Chicano Studies in the nation, which I didn't know at the time.

I talked to my constituents who were part of the anti-war movement, farm workers movement, and the Southern civil rights movement. I began thinking more and more about how we have got to start making our own revolution. What steps do we take? How do we do that? I thought about the schools as the target of the emerging movement. "Look at the schools," I said, "the schools are the reason that I and most of you here today could not go to a four-year college." That was number one. Number who was we got brainwashed.

At that time, I was not quite there in terms of understanding paradigms of colonization and internal colonization. I said we got brainwashed into so-called assimilation types of training and education. And we have got to take on the high schools because the schools are responsible for the perpetuation of us as a cheap labor force. So, we began to put together a plan to take on the school system. We met Sal Castro, one of the school teachers there. I have to give him the credit he deserves. He began talking about the issues before we did. So, we joined hands.

We talked to him about it. "We're going to help you out with community actions against the schools."

## School Blowouts, Indictments

In March of 1968, we pulled it off. Thousands of kids walked out of their high schools, which were primarily barrio schools located in East Los Angeles. So, I was a first-year graduate student who got involved in organizing the student strikes in high schools we called the "blow outs." That was sort of our secret key. We yelled outside the windows of their high schools, "Blow out! Blow out! We've got to walk out." So the kids would say we have got to walk out.

Thirteen of us including myself were arrested and indicted for organizing the blow outs. So there I was in the cell with these guys who were accused of actual felony crimes you are used to hearing about. Murder, bank robberies, drugs, rape. I was charged with conspiracy to disrupt the school system and after explaining to the guys in the cell what I was in for, they couldn't believe it. They said, "Wait a minute. You organized nonviolent strikes and you are here?" They wanted me to explain. I said, "You know what, it's a complicated story. A long, complicated story. I can't tell you in a few words in cell. I'd have to write a book about it." Up to that point, I had never thought about ever writing a book. But I began to give it serious thought at that point.

So, there I am in the cell, right? What am I going to do? What am I going to think? Am I going to be worried? Stressed out? I gotta relax and think about what am I going to do if I wind up in prison for 66 years. What am I going to do in prison for that long? I should begin to write a book. I should think about writing a book about why I am in prison. And I just remember now the guy who was in prison, George Jackson, a Black Panther you probably heard about. He was imprisoned and wrote a couple of books in prison. Another guy who became one of my heroes Antonio Gramsci from Italy. He was a communist during the Mussolini dictatorship in Italy and while imprisoned, he started writing a book called Prison Notebooks which I read in one of my college seminars. So, I started thinking that well, I can do what Jackson and Gramsci did if worse comes to worst. But I finally got out of prison because the ACLU and attorneys bailed me and the other guys out. I got out with a whole different goal in life.

I had become very critical. One of the reasons I thought we should demand a Mexican-American studies department was because of the lack of curriculum about our experiences as a people. We were invisible as a people. No one knew about Mexican-Americans except that they were immigrants and cheap labor. We as Mexican-Americans didn't know our history or what we thought about ourselves. So, we needed to come up with a curriculum which is another reason that I wanted to create a Chicano Studies department.

When I got out on bail, I thought well, in order for me to do that book, I think what I'm going to do is develop Chicano studies or Mexican-American studies in a way that I won't be the only one who will be able to write a book. To try to spread the thinking that we can be organic intellectuals as Gramsci wrote about. Gramsci was very key to me, as was Fanon, in terms of eventually coming up with the internal colonial model for my dissertation. I began to look at my experience in the military where I was stationed in the Third World. I saw with my own eyes what happens in the Third World, at least in Korea and Vietnam. I studied what happened in Mexico in the Mexican revolution that my grandfather was involved with. I studied the Cuban revolution. I studied what was going on in Africa and learned about Kwame Nkrumah and all these people who were fighting against Imperialist nations and colonizing nations. By the time I was able to get into the PhD program, I had an idea of what I wanted to do to develop a new paradigm.

(Carlos Munoz, Jr is professor emeritus in Chicano Studies and Ethnic Studies, UC Berkeley)

*Sather Gate. January February 1969. Doug Wachter photo.*

## Disseminating a New Perspective on Relevant Education

*TWLF information table on Sproul Plaza. January February 1969. Doug Wachter photo.*

*TWLF informational picket on Sproul Plaza. January February 1969. Doug Wachter photo.*

## Marching Through Classroom on North Campus

*February 1969. Doug Wachter photo.*

## Daily Informational Pickets on South Campus

*Picket sign: "Power to the People" Bancroft and Telegraph. February 1969. Doug Wachter photo.*

## Striker Wearing Button: "Self-Determination"

*Bancroft and Telegraph. February 1969. Doug Wachter photo*

## TWLF Mass Meeting

*Strike meeting. UC Berkeley campus. Doug Wachter photo.*

# MASC & the UFW Grape Boycott at Cal

*MANUEL RUBEN DELGADO*

Left: Manuel Delgado. Right: Richard Aoki, Charles Brown, Manuel Delgado. February 7, 1969. Muhammad Speaks.

At our first MASC (Mexican American Students Confederation) meeting of the academic year, we were told that members, led by Ralph Arreola, had been in negotiation with Scott Wilson, the business manager of student housing, to support the Delano Grape Boycott by not purchasing grapes for the dormitory dining halls. At a follow-up meeting with Don Campbell, Director of Purchasing and Finance, they had agreed to stop purchasing grapes. This had all been done without any public knowledge.

While I was in Mexico City, MASC had been busy on campus unknowingly laying groundwork for our next confrontation with the University.

Sid also reported that the university had agreed to let us interview for the new co-director of the Educational Opportunity Program. After introducing eleven new members we held elections for the fall quarter. I was elected Chairman and Ralph Arreola was elected Vice-Chairman.

The MASC victory in getting the university to support the Grape Boycott was short-lived. On Friday, October 4, we got word that grapes were still being served in the cafeterias. We quickly organized a protest on the steps of Sproul Hall demanding that the university stop purchasing scab grapes. Ralph Arreola and Tony Cedillo met later that day with Wilson and Campbell and got them to sign an agreement stating that they would honor the grape boycott.

Then on October 11, we got word that President Charles J. Hitch, who had just taken office in January, had reversed the policy initiated by Scott Wilson. We called an emergency meeting for that weekend. Ralph Arreola angrily waved the signed agreement with Scott Wilson and Campbell.

"They can't do this!" he yelled. "We have a signed agreement right here."

"But Hitch is claiming that they didn't have the authority," said Tony Cedillo.

"Well, I think we should do something," replied Arreola. "What do you think Manuel? You're the chairman."

"I think we should go over to Hitch's office and demand that he meet with us," I answered.

"But what if he's not there, or he puts us off?" Sid broke in. "We'll look foolish."

"We're not going to take no for an answer," Delgado said. "If he's not in or if he refuses to see us, we'll sit in."

"That means we might be arrested. Are we all willing to take that chance?" Sid asked.

"Let's decide right now who's willing to be arrested," I replied. "The rest of you can decide when the time comes."

I raised my hand first, followed by Sid, Fernando Garcia and Salomon Quintero.

"Orale," Delgado said. "Let's put our demands on paper."

Ralph repeated the original demand that the university not purchase scab grapes.

"Let's raise the ante," Delgado said. "If we're going to be arrested, let's make it worth our while. Let's include a demand that the university provide scholarships for the children of all farm workers."

"Let's include a demand for an increase in special admissions from four percent to ten percent," added Richard Rodriguez.

"How about a Chicano Study Center," added Sid.

"Como son cabrones," Delgado laughed. "Anything else?"

"That's it for now. If he turns down these demands, we'll add more," replied Salomon.

"Let's make some handouts announcing a demonstration at Hitch's office on 3pm Monday that includes our list of demands," Delgado said.

"I'll pass them around campus," offered Jaime Soliz.

"I'll call some community leaders and tell them what we're up to," added Richard Rodriguez.

At 3pm on Monday we started our walk to University Hall on Oxford Street. We took the elevator up to Hitch's office.

"Good afternoon," I said. "We'd like to see President Hitch."

"Do you have an appointment?" asked the receptionist.

"No we don't, but it's urgent that we see him now," I answered.

"I'll see if he has time to see you."

The receptionist went into another office and returned after a while.

"President Hitch is not going to be available this afternoon," she said. "Can I make you an appointment for another day?"

"No, we have to see him today. We'll just wait here in the lobby," I answered. "We'll stay here all night if necessary."

While we waited, another group of students joined us. Charles Palmer, who was elected ASUC President in May, and law students, Dan Siegel and Steve Bingham, were among the ones who joined. Charlie, who claimed to be half Chicano, would later go to Vietnam as President of the National Students Association and, while there, lead a protest against the war. Dan Siegel would lead the People's Park protest the following summer. And three years later, Steve Bingham would be charged with smuggling a gun to George Jackson for a San Quentin breakout attempt and charged with the deaths of two convicts and three guards.

By this time more than twenty people had gathered in the lobby including a few gringas. Before long, University Police Sergeant Robert R. Ludden came in and told us we had to leave.

"We're not leaving, officer, until President Hitch talks to us," I said.

"We've already closed off the entrance to the building and I've called for reinforcements. You have about ten minutes to get your stuff together and leave peacefully or you'll all be arrested for trespassing," he warned.

After a few minutes Earl C. Bolton, Vice President for Governmental Affairs, came in and asked what it was we wanted to see President Hitch about.

"We're here to protest Hitch's decision to reverse the agreement we had with Scott Wilson to stop the purchase of scab grapes. We demand to see President Hitch about this," I said.

"He's very busy right now but let me see if he has time to meet with you."

Bolton emerged from Hitch's office with a prepared statement:

"The University, as a public institution, is designed to serve all the people of California and should not discontinue the furnishing of any food products as a policy decision."

"That's not acceptable," I said. "We demand to see President Hitch now."

Bolton again went into Hitch's office. When he came back out, he said, "President Hitch is willing to talk to you about this but only for a few minutes."

I went in along with Sid Macias, Salomon Quintero, Fernando Garcia, Malaquias Montoya, and Richard Rodriguez. President Hitch was sitting behind a huge desk. We all smiled at each other. This was the President of one of the biggest and most prestigious universities in the world and he was barely visible beyond his huge desk.

"Mr. Hitch, we have an agreement signed by Scott Wilson, business manager for student housing, saying that he would no longer purchase scab grapes for the dining halls. Why did you rescind this agreement?" I asked.

"First, Mr. Wilson did not have the authority to make that kind of decision. You have to understand that the university is a public institution and cannot take sides in a labor dispute. The only reason we can legitimately stop buying grapes is if there is no demand for them. We can't side with the Farmworkers Union or the growers," he said.

"Mr. Hitch, by buying scab grapes you are taking sides. You can't have it both ways," I answered. "By allowing the University to purchase grapes you're using public money to support the rich growers in their attempt to crush the aspirations of the Mexican American people."

"Look, I'm sympathetic with the plight of the farm workers, but as President, I cannot allow the University to take sides in a public controversy which does not directly affect its own welfare," he answered.

"I think you're lying," said Richard Rodriguez. "We know that Earl Coate, Reagan's Agriculture Secretary, and Max Rafferty, State Superintendent of Public Instruction, pressured you into rescinding this agreement."

"We think you're a coward, President Hitch," yelled Sid. "You just don't have the courage to do what's right. We demand that you honor this agreement signed by Scott Wilson."

"And we also want you to agree to these other demands," I added. "We want scholarships for the children of farm workers; we want an increase in special admissions for underrepresented minorities and we want a Chicano Center with a budget to develop courses in Chicano history and culture."

"The University has a responsibility to serve all the people of California and we were here before you racists stole this land from Mexico," added Sid.

"I will take these demands under consideration but right now I have to leave," replied Hitch.

Then President Hitch rushed towards a side door in his office. Infuriated, I ran over and blocked him and slammed the door shut, for a moment forgetting I was no longer in the barrio.

"You're not leaving this room until you agree to these demands," I said.

Everyone understood the gravity of the situation before I did. Richard came over and whispered in my ear,

"Goddamn you Manuel, you went too far. You've just taken Hitch as a hostage. You've got to let him go."

Meanwhile Hitch was standing next to the side door looking frail and scared. I leaned over and opened the door for him. There was a collective sigh of relief. Then we all started laughing.

"Eres cabrón ese," sighed Salomon.

Sid opened the door leading to the reception area and let everybody in.

"What happened in there?" asked Charlie Palmer.

"He walked out on us," I answered.

Then Officer Ludden came in and announced, "This is now an unlawful assembly. If you do not leave immediately you will be arrested for trespassing."

"No entendemos Ingles Senor. El tratado de Guadalupe Hidalgo nos da el derecho de tener un intérprete," Sid replied.

We didn't really know that much about the Treaty of Guadalupe Hidalgo except that it guaranteed the civil rights of Mexicans who chose to remain in the newly acquired territory after the Mexican American War. None of us had actually read the Treaty but it was an opportunity to assert our rights as Mexicans. Ralph Arreola translated what Sid had said to Officer Ludden.

"They said that under the Treaty of Guadalupe they have a right to an interpreter."

"You tell these so-called Mexicans that I will return with an interpreter and then if they don't leave they, and everybody else out here in the reception area, will be arrested."

After Ludden left, we talked about who was going to stay and get arrested. Sid Macias, Sal Quintero, Fernando Garcia, Richard Rodriguez, Thelma Barrios, Nannette Kripke, Dorothy Jacobson, Shelley Safran, Dan Siegel, Steve Bingham and I volunteered to stay and get arrested.

"Orale, everybody else has to leave now," I said. "We're going to need every one of you to help build support on campus and to keep this is in the public eye."

After the others left, and before the Campus Police came in to arrest us, we made telephone calls to other student organizations around the state. We spoke to Rosalio Munoz, President of the United Mexican American Students at UCLA, and urged him to organize a demonstration at the UCLA campus in support of our action and for our demands. This was the first political action of this kind taken by a Chicano student organization in California and we were not sure how much support we would get. Rosalio was not encouraging. He told us he didn't think he could organize a demonstration on his campus in time to help. We would find out later that the students at UCLA considered us to be too "intellectual and Marxist oriented" to be taken seriously.

Finally, the police came in with an interpreter after which we were put under arrest. As we were taken out of the building, we were greeted by more than fifty demonstrators, with cheers and shouts of "Viva La Raza," and "Chicano Power." It was the first "mass arrests" at UC since the Free Speech Movement in 1966. Among the MASC members who had left Hitch's office before the arrests were Manuel Gomez, Ludi Tapia and Paz Flores from Cal State Hayward. More importantly there were Mexicans, Latinos and other Chicanos from campus who had not been to any of our meetings.

From University Hall we were taken to the Berkeley City Jail where we all spent the night. The next morning, we were taken to the Albany-Berkeley Municipal Court for arraignment. Waiting for us were over 150 students demonstrating outside the Courthouse.

> We could hear them singing "La Cucaracha."
>> La cucaracha, la cucaracha
>> Ya no puede caminar
>> Porque no tiene, porque le falta
>> Marijuana que fumar.

"La Cucaracha" is the Spanish equivalent of "Yankee Doodle." It's a traditional satirical tune whose words were changed to meet the needs of the moment. It is said that the song was used by the Spanish in the war against the Moros (Muslims) and by Pancho Villa Against the Huertistas during the Mexican Revolution. The Cockroach refers to the adversary; in this case it was President Hitch.

Robert E. Gonzalez, an attorney from Oakland, volunteered to represent us. He got Thelma Barrios, Nan Kripke, Dorothy Jacobson and Shelley Sarfan released on their own recognizance. We told Mr. Gonzalez that we planned to stage a hunger strike until our demands were met. I asked him for a piece of paper so I could leave instructions for the members who were demonstrating outside.

The instructions were to add two more demands to the list we left with President Hitch: total amnesty for the eleven of us and a promise to recruit 400 Chicanos for the 1969-1970 academic year. After the arraignment the rest of us were transferred to the Alameda County Correctional Facility in Santa Rita.

At our first mess call we sat down with the other prisoners without getting into the food line. "What's your problem?" asked a guard. "We don't serve you here. Get in the food line."

"We're not eating," I said. "We're on a hunger strike."

The guards immediately took us back to our beds and told us, "If you're not going to eat don't go to the mess hall. Just stay here. We don't want you inciting a riot in there."

After two days without food Sid started talking about how good it would be to have a couple of tacos or enchiladas.

"Tu y tus pinches tacos ese. Stop talking about food," I said.

"How about some milk, at least?" he asked.

"No tacos, no enchiladas and no milk, just water," I answered.

"I could handle this if I knew what the hell was going on out there," added Fernando. "No parece que están haciendo nada. They're going to let us rot in here."

"Maybe one of us should post bail to see what's going on out there," said Richard.

"Let's wait another day to see what happens. We've already committed ourselves to this. We can't back out now," I answered.

On the third day, October 17, a trustee came in to tell me I had a visitor.

"Someone named Lepawsky," he said.

It was the professor from my Senior Honors Seminar.

"Ask him to bail you out so you can light a fire under those people out there," said Sid.

I was escorted to the visitor's center and told to wait. I could see Professor Lepawsky in the visitor's room. He was a really good person and he cared about his students. I felt really guilty about how we treated him in our class on Public Policy and Planning.

"I just talked to your wife, Manuel. She's really worried about you. She had no idea you were so involved in this Chicano cause."

"It's something we had to do, Professor. We Chicanos don't know how to back down. Respect is a big thing with us and we believe President Hitch disrespected us when he rescinded the agreement we had with Scott Wilson."

"Well I don't want you in here Manuel. I think it's more important for you to be at home with your family. I'm ready to put up bail for you right now."

"I don't think I can do that Professor, at least not until I talk to my friends."

"Go talk to them. It's a long way to Berkeley and back so I'll wait here."

I already knew what the guys would say since they were desperate to know what was happening on campus. It was the first time any of them had been arrested. I had already been arrested six times in San Bernardino.

"Quien era, Manuel?"

"It was one of my professors. He wants to bail me out."

"What did you tell him?"

"I told him I couldn't do that without talking to you."

"Let him, ese. I don't think those guys out there know what they're doing. You've got to go and negotiate a settlement with the university."

"Does everybody feel the same about this?" I asked.

"Yeah, we all feel the same," they answered.

Lepawsky and I left Santa Rita around 3 PM and arrived in Berkeley around 4:30. Professor Lepawsky took me home and told me, "I'll see you tonight at my house," he said, "for the seminar. I'm sure the other students will be very interested in your political adventure. They might even be willing to help in some way."

As soon as I got inside the apartment I was rushed by little Marky and my dog Maurice. After dinner, we sat down and talked about what had happened. I told Nena I had to prepare a speech that I was sure I was going to be asked to give the next day, probably on the steps of Sproul Hall. We worked late into the night on a speech that was modeled after the one Father Miguel Hidalgo gave to his congregation of Indians and Mestizos on September 16, 1812, in the village of Dolores, declaring Mexico's independence from Spain. I was going to end the speech the same way -- by calling out "Mexicanos, Viva Mexico."

The next day I went to the MASC office to see what had occurred while we were in Santa Rita. The guys had really misjudged the MASC members. Under the leadership of Ralph Arreola, MASC had mobilized a mass demonstration at the Albany-Berkeley Courthouse on the 15th. Afterwards they held a press conference where they defended the sit-in and the purpose of the hunger strike. Charlie Palmer, ASUC President, told the press that the sit-in was a result of the university's decision not to support the Grape Boycott, and the purpose of the hunger strike was to reaffirm our dedication to non-violent civil disobedience. Ralph Arreola had read the letter I had given our Attorney after being arraigned.

"Mexican Americans are underrepresented on this campus. Therefore, we demand the immediate enrollment of 400 Chicanos to correct the situation."

"And we further demand total amnesty for the Chicano Eleven."

After the press conference 500 students had marched over to University Hall demanding that Hitch meet with representatives of the Mexican American Student Confederation. Later that day Public Information Officer Richard Hafner announced,

"The Berkeley campus will continue not to serve grapes in the residence hall cafeterias. We do not consider this to be in violation of President Hitch's policy statement of 'not getting involved in the grape boycott.'"

In just nine months the Mexican American Student Confederation had forced changes in the Educational Opportunity Program that would increase the number of Chicanos participating to fifty percent. It had gotten the Berkeley campus to support the Delano Grape Boycott and to establish a Chicano Center.

(Manuel Ruben Delgado was a member of the Mexican American Students Confederation [MASC] and a veteran of the 1969 TWLF Strike at UC Berkeley)

# The Wisdom of a College Structure

*MEXICAN AMERICAN STUDENTS CONFEDERATION (MASC) 1969*

A separate college is herein recommended as the most suitable vehicle for a Third World studies program, for the following reasons:

Most existing university faculties and departments have had a century or more to develop multi-ethnic approaches to history, art, literature, education, etc., but they have been largely unable to do so… these same faculties cannot now be expected to do what they have in the past rejected or failed to consider as "academically worthy" subjects.

- The area of Third World studies and inter-ethnic analysis has suffered from the fact that disciplines theoretically concerned with this field (sociology, anthropology, psychology, etc.) have tended to develop highly specialized methodologies or approaches which have seldom allowed for a systematic, interdisciplinary focus on problems of ethnicity as such.
- A Third World studies program, to be meaningful, must embrace basic research (theoretical as well as empirical), applied research, and extensive field training. Because of these factors such a program does not belong in the College of Letters and Sciences. Basic research cannot, however, be ignored since so many of the needs of Third World peoples cannot be fully met until tools are available.
- The faculty for a Third World studies program will have to possess varying kinds of expertise. Many will doubtless be persons who could qualify for appointments in the College of Letters and Sciences, but others will be practitioners comparable to faculties of Schools of Education, Law, etc. The doctorate does not make a person qualified to teach in the area of Native American Community Development, for example.
- The distinction between a "School" and a "College" according to the Standing Orders of the Regents precludes the establishment of "School" since a "School" may not enroll lower-division students.

# Introduction to "Proposal for Establishing a Black Studies Program"

*LETTER FROM THE AFRO-AMERICAN STUDENTS UNION TO THE DAILY CAL IN 1968*

*The Afro-American Students Union (AASU) initiated formation of TWLF at UC Berkeley. Doug Wachter photos.*

The young Black people of America are inheritors of what is undoubtedly one of the most challenging, gravest, and threatening set of social circumstances that has ever fallen upon a generation of young people anywhere in history. We have been born into a hostile and alien society which loathes us on condition of our skin color. Our intimidated and frightened parents, not less but more victimized, have been unable to tell us why. Sentenced to inanes, subservience, and death, from our beginning, many of us came to regard our beautiful pigmentation as a plague. It should surprise no one that the first thing we discovered was our "souls," as we were so bare and totally lacking anything else. Unless there be a reason for misunderstanding — let us make it clear that we neither cry nor complain to anyone about being left with our souls because the soul is sufficient unto itself. We act now because we realize, beyond any doubt, that our "souls," because the soul is sufficient unto itself. We act now because we realize, beyond any doubt, that our "souls", i.e., that which is all and the end of us, has been stifled to the point that we can no longer bear it. We have been forced to the point where we must (and will) insist on those changes that are necessary to our survival. There is nothing less to settle for and nothing less will do.

The college and university campuses of America are a long way from where most of us come. Our homeland (known to white folks as the GHETTO) is hardly conducive to growing ivy. "Mother wits was our thing, not encyclopedias. We have been the companions of every evil, cycle, syndrome, or mania that would strike fear in the hearts of our white compatriots. Those of us who survive have seen everything but the end. This many of us stayed by trekking from our homeland to your midst; to your college and university campuses. We could not have imagined what awaited us.

As students on the white college and university campuses of America we have learned something which we choose never to forget.

WE ARE NOT WHITE. WE DO NOT WISH TO BE WHITE. WHAT IS GOOD FOR WHITE PEOPLE IS OFTENTIMES WORSE THAN BAD FOR US.

Education in America, as we have come to know it, is a strictly utilitarian endeavor. The colleges and universities have not been established for the sake of education. The colleges and universities are the wholesale producers of a designated mentality conducive to the perpetuation and continuation of America's present national life. A national life which we have witnessed to be in total and complete contradiction to the wholesome development and survival of our people. There is little need to detail the sad circumstances of our plight in American society. This tale is already well known. But even the blind and insane could deny or refute the unspeakable horrors that America has wrought upon its citizens of color. Finally, we have witnessed white America's long overdue self-admittance of its racism. Thus, knowing and recognizing fully the gravity of the circumstances under which we labor, we are moving to institute all those change perquisite to our survival in an openly hostile country.

"YOUR EDUCATION IS ON THE LINE!!"

*Afro-American Students Union (AASU) members leading TWLF march through UC Berkeley campus. Winter 1968. Doug Wachter photo.*

# Black Panther Party Platform was first to introduce Ethnic Studies concept. October 1966.

> **5. WE WANT** education for our people that exposes the true nature of this decadent American society. We want education that teaches us our true history and our role in the present-day society.
>
> WE BELIEVE in an educational system that will give to our people knowledge of self. If a man does not have knowledge of himself and his position in society and the world, then he has little chance to relate to anything else.

*From Black Panther Party Ten Point Platform & Program. October 1966. Credits: itsabouttimebpp.com*

*Black Panther Party office in Oakland, CA., circa 1960s. Credits: itsabouttimebpp.com*

*Origins & Background*

# Bureau of Indian Affairs (BIA) Relocation Policies

*LaNada War Jack recounts moving to San Francisco*[52]

SF State and UC Berkeley and other Native Americans occupy Alcatraz. Left: LaNada War Jack. Ramparts Magazine.

By then I was eighteen years old, I was lucky to be sent by the BIA to the boarding home of Mrs. Margaret Pascale in San Francisco. . . I wound up running the place with Mrs. Pascale, and we boarded up to thirty girls coming out on relocation. She had a huge, beautiful home on the first avenue near the park. Next to my own mother, I loved her dearly.

Others and I began our new lifestyles in the cities and socialized primarily with our own people. It was easy to divide Natives against Natives on the reservations, but when you are in a major city, you're so glad to see another Native that you don't care what tribe a Native is from, other than a curiosity because it doesn't make any difference. You are all Natives and that is all that counts."

. . . we decided to protest the BIA in San Francisco and Oakland regarding how the relocation program dropped young reservation Indians off in the cities without much support a return ticket. We wanted the BIA to assist us with our educational goals rather than just vocational schools and employment. We wanted to go to the Bay Area colleges and universities.

---

52  Excerpt from: Native Resistance: An Intergenerational Fight for Survival and Life. Dr. LaNada War Jack. Donning: 2019.

. . . our comments about the BIA did not sit well with the federal government. They did not want to support our educational goals, and they suddenly dropped the relocation program.

*LaNada War Jack (4th from left) and Family Members at Multicultural Community Center, UC Berkeley. November 21, 2019. Harvey Dong photo*

# The Student Population to be Served by Indian Studies[53]

## UNITED NATIVE AMERICANS (1969)

It is quite clear that the programs of most colleges and universities in the United States have been, and still are, oriented towards serving the white middle-class or upper-class populations. These programs have never prepared Indian students for adquate participation in the ongoing development of Indian communities, and, in addition, their anti-Indian bias has served to alienate those native students who have managed to overcome the hurdles posed by white secondary education and pro-white admission procedures.

Clearly, then, any college which hopes to serve Indian students must develop a comprehensive Indian Studies program.

The rationale for established such a program does not consist solely in meeting the needs of Indian students however. Many non-Indians will continue to earn their livings by working with native populations as teachers and other professionals. These people have often performed dismally in the past and their training must be radically altered.

Finally, and perhaps most significantly of all, a massive effort must be made by colleges and universities to overcome the chauvinism, ethnocentrism, and narrow nationalism of the Anglo-American people. This can only occur, in so far as higher education is concerned, when college faculties overcome their own chauvinism and create truly multicultural and multi-ethnic institutions.

The development of Native American Studies, along with Black Studies, Asian Studies, and Mexican American/Latin American Studies, is clearly an essential and overdue step in that direction.

**Specific Course Proposals**
  Native American Literature
  American Indian Legal-Political Studies
  Native American Arts
  Native American Religion and Philosophy
  Native American Education
  American Indian Languages
  American Indian Tribal and Community Development

---

53  TWLF Newspaper "Solidarity." March 4, 1969. P. 5.

## Patty Silva authored first Native American Studies Course Proposal

*Patty Silva at TWLF Reunion at Multicultural Community Center. October 6, 2018. Harvey Dong photo.*

*Origins & Background*

# Understanding AAPA (Asian American Political Alliance)

*AAPA Newspaper Summer 1969*

*Asian American Political Alliance (AAPA) members conducting strike activities. January 1969. Doug Wachter photo.*

We Asian Americans believe that we must develop an American society which is just, humane, equal, and gives the people the right to control their lives before we can begin to end the oppression and inequality that exists in this nation.

We Asian Americans realize that America was always and still is a White Racist Society. Asian Americans have been continuously exploited and oppressed by the racist majority and have survived only through hard work and resourcefulness, but their souls have not survived.

We Asian Americans refuse to cooperate with the White Racism in this society which exploited us as well as other Third World people; and affirm the right of Self-Determination.

We Asian Americans support all oppressed peoples and their struggles for Liberation and believe that Third World People must have complete control over the political, economic and educational institutions within their communities.

We Asian Americans oppose the imperialistic policies being pursued by the American Government.[54]

Yellow Symposium sponsored by AAPA, Chinese Students Club and Nisei Students Club of UC Berkeley. website: aam1968.blogspot.com

---

54  Asian Community Center Archive Group. Stand Up: An Archive Collection of the Bay Area Asian American Movement, 1968-1974. (Eastwind Books of Berkeley, 2009), p. 30.

## "Unity is our Strongest Weapon. Unite Join the Strike" (TWLF picket sign)

*AAPA members on picket duty. January February 1968. Doug Wachter photo.*

*AAPA members and others on Sproul Plaza. January February 1968. Doug Wachter photo.*

### BERKELEY HISTORY
# ASIAN AMERICAN MOVEMENT BIRTHPLACE

By the late 1960s, a new generation of political activists emerged in Berkeley from protests opposing the Vietnam War and supporting the Farmworkers, Free Speech, and Civil Rights movements. In May 1968, in an apartment on this site, Yuji Ichioka and others founded the Asian American Political Alliance (AAPA). AAPA sparked the nationwide Asian American Movement: uniting Americans previously divided by ethnicity— Filipino, Japanese, Korean, Chinese, and others—and stereotyped as "Orientals" or "silent minorities."

AAPA joined African American, Latino, and Native American groups in the Third World Liberation Front, which led the 1969 Third World Strike at UC Berkeley. The strikes here and elsewhere spurred the creation of ethnic studies and social justice programs and encouraged community self-determination.

*This plaque was placed to commemorate the 50th anniversary of AAPA and the Asian American Movement.*

*Berkeley Historical Plaque Project 2018*

*Origins & Background*

# Remarks of Prof. Paul Takagi. 1969

### REMARKS OF DR. PAUL TAKAGI*

Let me sit down and talk about "Yellow Identity." It first came to public attention at the YELLOW IDENTITY SYMPOSIUM on the Berkeley campus in January of this year. But before that, in November, 1968, the Chinese, Japanese, and Filipino students at Berkeley asked me if I would sponsor a course in Asian Studies and I said that I would. The students wanted not to learn about their Asian culture, but something about what it means to be an Asian in America. The course was approved by the Board of Educational Development at the University, sponsored as an experimental course in Winter Quarter 1969, and during the pre-registration some 70 students showed up. We were somewhat apprehensive about the student response, but on the first day of the lecture, 150 students enrolled for the course and during the rest of the quarter some 200 to 225 people, including some of the members of the community, participated in lectures. Since then, UC Davis and UCLA have started Asian American Studies courses based, I think, partly upon our experiences in Berkeley. In addition, I have had people from USC inquire about the course, from Stanford, UC Santa Cruz, the local State Colleges and even Junior Colleges.

What I would like to do today is to analyze why students respond so enthusiastically to the concept of Asian American Studies. And secondly to analyze how is it or why is it that the concept has gained acceptance so rapidly. For example, earlier last week I was in Chicago and my sister had asked that I stop and talk to her church group at her house. There were 30 people, scared. They thought that the students of the West Coast had a severe social problem; that they were raising hell at San Francisco State and UC Berkeley, and they could not understand what was happening. I attempted to assure them that this was a real healthy movement. They were somewhat dubious but my niece decided at that time, a 20-year-old college dropout, that she had to come to the Coast to see for herself. She has been visiting us for about ten days; hanging around the Asian American Political Alliance kids, and now she wants to go back to school. Now she feels that there is a purpose in going back to school.

Most of us in this room thought of college in terms of a self-instrumental objective; that is, we go to school and become an engineer, a pharmacist, a doctor, or a lawyer. But not these Asian kids on the campus now--not all of them. What they want to do is to go to school and learn content and after they have learned about the content, they want to learn a discipline. They want to become a technician secondly, but first they want to learn something about what it means to be a human being in this world today. In some respects, the interest in the Asian American Studies is a rebellion similar to the other major forms of rebellions that have occured in the United States during the past ten years: the violence in the urban ghetto; the movement of the New Left; the movement of the Radical Right in an effort to regain something that they will never be able to; the style rebellion in terms of costume, music, dance, art and the comedy; and finally, the so-called "hippie" or dropout rebellion. The Asian students on the campus, I think, are expressing the same kind of protest and the same sense of frustration. What I would like to do here is to become a little more academic in an attempt to analyze the feelings and problems of Asian students. These, incidentally, are not unique to them, because, I think, we here in this room, have the same kinds of frustrations, the same kind of feelings. But we haven't really looked at ourselves in a way the younger generation have examined their own feelings.

---

*Presented at COMMUNITY SEMINAR: The Asian American Identity
Saturday, April 26, 1969
San Francisco, California

*Speech by Dr. Paul Takagi, Prof of Criminology and sponsor of first Asian American Studies class at UC Berkeley. 1969.*

# From Asian Studies Proposal. General Purpose and Principles

*Submitted by AAPA (1969)*

The Asian experience in America is unique. The lives of the Japanese, Chinese, Filipino, Korean, and other Asian people have similarities and differences, but generally fall under the category of the Yellow Experience. The phenomena of a colorful people living in a white society deserves study, understanding, and sensitive analysis. It deserves this study because these colorful people need it, in order to understand themselves and the society in which they live.

The effects of American and Western civilization on the non-Western world have been profound. From the earliest contacts of European explorers with the Chinese and Southeast Asians to the present-day Western military, economic, and political activities and spheres in Asia, the "white" man has been involved with the "yellow" man.

From the study of these two related experiences — Asians in America and Westerners in Asia — we can perhaps arrive at some understanding about the "yellow-white" relationship at its social and psychological roots and manifestations.

*Bancroft Avenue Picket. January 1969. Doug Wachter photo.*

# Chapter Two:
# Strike Reflections

*West Campus. 1969. Doug Wachter photo.*

# Black, Brown, Red, Yellow & White. All the People Must Unite!

*Doug Wachter Photography*

## Informational Picketting

*Informational pickets in early phases of the strike. January 1969. Doug Wachter photo.*

## TWLF Townhall

*TWLF Forum. left to right: Alan Fong and Don Davis. Pauley Ballroom. January 1969. Doug Wachter photo.*

## Strike Support Committee

A Strike Support Committee was established to include white students and more established movement organizations who were in support of the TWLF demands.

The TWLF was comprised of Asian, African American, Chicano and Native American student groups.

At different strike turning points, mass town hall meetings took place.

*January 1969. Doug Wachter photos.*

*Indoor forum in Pauley Ballroom. Right photo: Richard Aoki at podium. January 1969. Doug Wachter photos.*

## Teaching Assistants Union Support TWLF Demands

*On February 13, 1969, the police completely surrounded and arrested 36 people from AFT 1570 (UC teaching assistants) who were picketing in support of the TWLF strike as well as their own union issues. Doug Wachter Photo.*

## UC Berkeley Staff Workers Union Support

UC staff workers union, American Federation of State, County and Municipal Employees (AFSCME) Local 1695 joined in support of the TWLF and teaching assistants strikes. January 1969. Doug Wachter photo.

*Strike Reflections*

*Upper left: Sign: "Strike in Living Color" Other photos: campus support events. Winter 1969. Doug Wachter photos*

*Strike pamphlet in response to increased presences of police in Sather Gate area. January 1969. TWLF Graphic.*

*Picket captain Cordell Abercrombie. Doug Wachter photos.*

*Police clearing Sproul Plaza with tear gas. February 1969. Doug Wachter photos.*

*Anticipation over increased police presence on campus. February 1969. Doug Wachter photos.*

*Top: Crowds forced onto Telegraph. Bottom: Police march through campus. February 1969. Doug Wachter photos.*

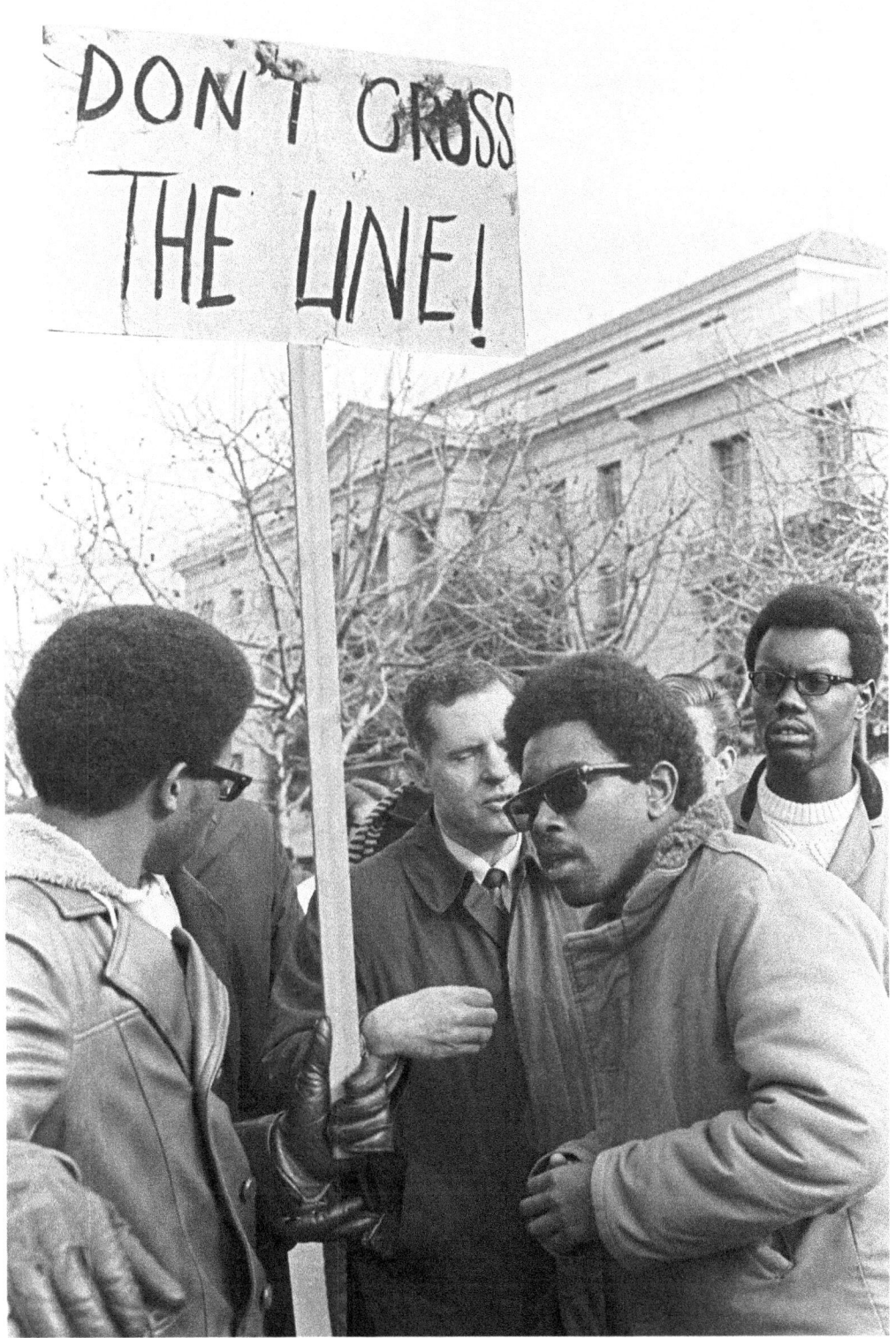

*Strike sign calling for solidarity: "Don't Cross the Line." February 1969. Doug Wachter photo.*

*Pickets on Bancroft and Telegraph, South Campus. February 1969. Doug Wachter photos.*

*Strike Reflections*

*March near Campanile. February 1969. Doug Wachter photos.*

*Bancroft and Telegraph pickets during winter rain. February 1969. Doug Wachter photos.*

# The Strike Escalates

*YSIDRO MACIAS*

*Excerpts from an interview with Ysidro Macias. Interview by Harvey Dong, 2018.*

*March Down Bancroft Avenue. Left to right: Charles Brown of AASU, Ysidro Macias of MASC, LaNada Means of NASU, and Stan Kadani of AAPA. (Chicano Studies Program Records, Ethnic Studies Library, UC Berkeley, CS ARC 2009/1, Carton 1, Folder 14.)*

The Governor of California, Ronald Reagan, was a well-known white supremacist. The guy had been very clear about his view that minorities were here to serve the interests of white people. My wife's uncle's in fact was his gardener at one time when the guy lived in Bel-Air. So, I knew from talking to my wife's uncle later on that Ronald Reagan was consistent in how he treated minorities. He (Reagan) just felt that he was privileged being a white person, so he was the one that was pushing for resistance against the concept of Ethnic Studies, not only against San Francisco State but also when we declared our strike in Berkeley.

Initially, the activity on the picket line was on the slow side. At the beginning, the first couple of days, there was considerable enthusiasm. But people's enthusiasm and conviction started waning a little bit. Then all of a sudden, a week or two weeks into the strike, there was a fire at Wheeler Auditorium.

. . and the buzz was that the Third World Liberation Front had set fire to the Wheeler Auditorium . . . that we were determined to burn it down.

I don't know who did that fire. I know the bottom line though was the gossip that the Third World Liberation Front meant business. That it would be willing to be violent or be aggressive in attaining ethnic studies classes. I think this was the first impact on the regular student body.

After that fire in the Wheeler Auditorium, we decided that we were no longer gonna be nice on the picket line. We had been picketing on Bancroft Way right at the entrance of the Sproul Plaza which was a highly congested area. Most of the students that were not picketing would go around us and essentially honored our picket line. But there were some assholes, as there always is, who just took special pleasure in walking right through our picket lines as if they were gonna show us that we couldn't deny them their education.

We decided we were gonna get tough on these ones who decided to break our picket line and that's what we did. When they broke through, we went straight after those assholes and beat the shit out of them. This went on for about two or three days. Then the jocks and the engineers found out that we were beating up white ass, they decided to come with their bully ways to try and take on these small Asians and Mexicans. . . because most of the people on the picket line quite frankly were Asians and Chicanos. Even though the African American student group was as large or larger than the Asians, I think they had over 300 members, there was only like no more than three or four blacks on the picket line then. Don Davis was one of them and I remember Jim Nabors. They were there pretty much all the time.

So when the jocks and the engineers came, they decided that they were gonna beat us up and show us who was boss. But they found out that we meant business and we ended up kicking their ass too. This went on for a couple of days and all of a sudden, Governor Reagan started calling on the Berkeley City police initially, and the San Leandro or whatever East Bay police departments to come onto campus and try to quell our strike.

They (the police) were essentially passive until the later inclusion of the Alameda County deputies which were really aggressive law enforcement types, the ones we call the Blue Meanies. After the confrontation with the jocks and the engineers, the Blue Meanies came on campus They started beating up students and being aggressive with students. A lot of white students who previously had either ignored or were against the strike, started getting upset because they felt they were being harassed by the police.

They didn't want to see the increased police presence on campus and so they started actually supporting our strike and of course the most helpful aid came from the radical white students who volunteered and were willing to raise money, do leafleting and stuff like that. They wanted to be in the picket line as well but we were determined that this was going to be done by people of color, and even though we appreciated the white radical support we said no. On the picket line, it was to only be Third World people.

We later changed the policy. Since we had a significant amount of white student support, we might as well take advantage of this support. We came up with a concept known as the serpentine lines. The serpentine lines were essentially four students abreast and then the line would run 30 to 40 yards, probably maybe it was even longer. The serpentine line would go into a hall where classes were being held and we would just open the door and march through the front door. Usually these classrooms had a back door. It would effectively create like a slithering line of students that was disrupting these classes. There was always someone of our group who took the time to declare to the students who were seething that the reason their precious education was being disrupted was because we just wanted to have the same right they already had to take classes where they could study who they were and how they fit into the general scheme of society.

We used those serpentine lines to basically disrupt business as usual because we felt that was the only way we could get the attention of the mass population of students as to what we were after. The logic of what we were after was so simple and so elementary. It's something that I think should have been granted if not for the resistance from Ronald Reagan and his cohorts as things turned out.

## The Longest Sentence:

I was tried for felonious assault on a police officer because I had my foot struck his butt. I didn't know anything about the law back then, but luckily, I knew you don't do that to a so-called police officer.

But the fact that I was an Army veteran and I didn't have a criminal background other than my political activities, I thought it was okay I could skate away with some probation behind this shit. I mean, it's not like I hit the guy with a baton or aimed the gun at him or whatever.

However, what had apparently happened is the Alameda County District Attorney was Edwin Meese, who was later the Attorney General for Reagan when Reagan became president in 1980. Edwin Meese was a die-hard

Reaganite-nazi and he assigned the baddest pit bull that he had in his squadron of prosecutors to my case. I had a lawyer called John George, a really nice Black dude who later became the Alameda County supervisor and an assemblyman. He was well-connected but he couldn't do much. We were very fond of each other, but John – I called him JG – told me my case was his first criminal defense case ever. He wasn't very well versed in that field of defense. Eventually, they didn't offer anything, no deal, nothing.

They were intent on getting a conviction. It didn't take much time. No more than two hours after the jury went in, they came back with a felony conviction. I was kind of stunned. At the same time, I hadn't really grasped the significance of what that meant.

The judge gave me a month or so to come back for sentencing and when I returned, I received nine months right away and without hesitation. He specifically told me that he was going to make an example out of me and so without further bail or consideration, they handcuffed me and took me away to Santa Rita where I was going to be for nine months. I believe this was and still continues to be the longest sentence ever given to a student at UC Berkeley for any political activity associated with the campus.

So there I was in Santa Rita. About a year before, I had been jailed for the hunger strike and so I was somewhat used to that facility already. In jail, there were street Chicanos from Union City and Fremont, from Chicano barrios in Alameda County. They weren't students. They were hardcore guys. They already knew what was going in Berkeley, and for me to have been busted for kicking an Alameda County deputy in the butt… I mean, that was a badge of honor. So I fit in real well in the Chicano group at Santa Rita. Like I said, I had mentally prepared myself to spend nine months.

Fortunately, a committee of students collected some dollars to form a defense committee and to hire an attorney. They were able to hire Fay Stender, who was considered one of the top criminal defense attorneys in the Bay Area. At the time, her case involved defending Huey Newton from the Black Panther Party. Within a couple weeks of hiring her, she wrote and filed a brief with the appellate court. It was granted and bail was soon granted. So I had served about over two months when they suddenly informed me that I was out on bail. That's how I got out.

The date of that order from the appellate court was December 20, 1969. For several months of court appearances, I noticed there was another guy and formed a nodding relationship with him. On June 21, 1970, the guy was with a really sharp attorney. The attorney made a motion before the court and asked for a dismissal based upon the violation of the statute of limitations. The judge granted it to him, and the guy was free.

I was like, whoa! I hustled over to the guy and asked his lawyer to help JG out. Sure enough, the sharp lawyer asked the judge to reconvene the court. The lawyer walked JG through the motion. Soon, my conviction was wiped clean and I was scot free. That's how I said screw you to the legal system and got away from being a felon, which obviously would have affected me in terms of getting a job and barred me from voting. So that's how things developed for me in order to avoid a permanent conviction of my record.

*Returning 50 years later, TWLF members (left to right: Oliver Jones, Harvey Dong, Douglas Daniels, Steve Wong) meet at Sproul Steps. January 22, 2019. Keith Kojimoto Photo.*

## Joining the TWLF After Relocation

*LANADA WAR JACK*

Left: LaNada War Jack, H. Dong photo. Right: Police activity during TWLF Strike. January 1969. Doug Wachter photo.

In 1965, I left my home reservation on the Shoshone Bannock Tribes in Fort Hall, Idaho. I was on the Bureau of Indian Affairs (BIA) Relocation Program to one of the six largest cities in the U.S. as part of the governmental policy effort to "assimilate Indians into the mainstream of American Society." It was the BIA's intention to assist us to find employment or technical training. I came out on employment assistance but realized I wanted to attend a university. The university making the loudest sounds with protests and student activity was UC Berkeley.

Although I couldn't get assistance from the BIA to attend college since the program was only for employment or technical training, I decided to go anyways. I lived in the Mission District in San Francisco and I involved myself in the Native organizational activities. We all worked together with other groups, including an African American group called the Mission Rebels ran by the Reverend Jesse James. Reverend James had a UC Mission project which he was helping to place bright Black youth into the UC Berkeley Economic Opportunity Program (EOP). I made contact with Reverend James and asked if he could help me get into UC Berkeley. He contacted Dr. Andrew Billingsley at the EOP office, and I got admitted to the university on a probationary status until I could prove I could do the work. After my first quarter, I was off probation and a regular student.

In January 1968, I became the first Native American to attend the University of California through EOP. On campus, I met members of the Chicano organization who actively recruited me thinking that I was Mexican. I told them I was Indian, and they thought that was even better because they identified with their Native ancestry and highly respected Native people. With the support of my new friends and the EOP office, I was able to recruit other Native American students including my older brother and younger sister. As soon as we had several Native American students on campus, we set out to organize our own Native American Student organization on campus of which I became the chair. We were allowed space for our student office on campus and we maintained contact with the Indian community in the Bay Area. We believed institutionalization of our programs would allow us to educate not only ourselves but share our true history and culture with "mainstream American" where we were only known through movies and media's negative stereotypes.

By the fall of 1968, the Chicano organization informed me that the Black students were going on strike for Black studies and we had an opportunity to join in alliance for all our Ethnic Studies departments if we wanted. Of course, we wanted to see a thriving Black studies, Asian studies, Chicano Studies, Native American Studies, and Third World Studies departments.

This would be the best step to take because our cultural identity and survival as Indigenous people were being compromised within the educational mainstream of American through the continuing assimilation and acculturation process. It was a dilemma wanting to be educated on one hand but on the other hand, not wanting to become a poor carbon copy or a good Xerox of the white man. We were afraid of becoming brainwashed and programmed like the educated people who entered the system before us. For example, the "sell-out" natives working in the BIA against us at the time and inevitably taking our brightest youth to work in large corporations or in mining and oil industries, and so forth destroying the earth. Ignorance of our people fuels racism. The best place to combat that was through the education institution, thus the need for an Interdisciplinary Third World College.

The "Third World Strike" at Berkeley in 1969 was the most expensive Berkeley campus riots because they assembled the largest force of Berkeley police and National Guard. They marched on campus with their unsheathed bayonets and fogged the campus with pepper gas. Every class on campus was interrupted and stopped. All of the Third World leadership including myself were arrested during the strike for various alleged charges. When the gas cleared away, I was one of the coalition leaders on the four-man negotiation team advocating for our Third World college. We arose victorious with our own Department of Interdisciplinary Ethnic Studies which consisted of four departments within the university system. This was the very first Ethnic

Studies department in the UC campus statewide system which was replicated throughout California and the nation.

After the strike, we were busy drafting our studies proposals and initiating curriculum. I was on a six-month suspension for my involvement with the strike that semester but worked with Dr. Jack Forbes at Far West Research Laboratories in Berkeley who assisted in the development of the curriculum in conjunction with David Risling of the California Indian Education Association. We were able to call the first Native American Studies Curriculum Conference at UC Davis. The Third World Coalition asked for a Native American to head the Ethnic Studies Program, and the only one with a PhD I knew was Dr. Jack Forbes. I recommended him to our TWLF team, but him and David Risling believed the system would be too limiting and confining to work within. Dr. Forbes stepped down and named Lee Brightman the head. We were concerned that he did not consult with us in that selection. We probably would have agreed anyways but we saw that our input as students were taken away.

This was the first and last time in my lifetime that I ever experienced "Indian unity." As Indian students, we worked, studied, lived, played together, and helped and cared for each other as brothers and sisters. We were tight. We worked with all the Native organizations in the Bay Area and California with an emphasis on community/reservation-based curriculum. Prior to UC Berkeley's strike, San Francisco State University also went through a great campus upheaval to institute Third World Studies. Our campus organizations held joint meetings regularly and grew into one larger coalition of Native students. We planned most of our activities altogether including Pow Wows, conferences and meetings.

The Third World Strike at Berkeley was the last and most violent of all student protests and now it was over. Only when young people of color united in peaceful assemblies were we victorious, although we took some heavy hits. Afterwards, I felt bad about non-Natives being allowed to teach Native classes because they had tenure. This was not the intent and is a perpetuation of stereotypes, lies and mockery of our history and people. Non-natives do not possess the experiences of a Native person. We did also have had conflicts with Natives who assimilated and were products of the system with degrees from high-level universities. The intent was to create a level of truth in history, experience and understanding of the natural world. We didn't want the product of brainwashing to continue that legacy.

I would say unity was our success because we all worked together. I believed the future generations can continue to be successful by working together. Each leadership from each group must meet together regularly and students need to take a class from each of the departments. This way they can know the histories of each group and create friendships rather than staying isolated in their own respective groups. This needs to happen is we want to continue striving for a cohesive unity, strength and success.

*Aztec dance performance opening the TWLF 50th. January 22, 2019. Photo by Harvey Dong*

# I Am Who I Am Because of the Third World Strike

CLEMENTINA DURON

Left: Clementina Duron photo. Right: Strike photo by Doug Wachter. January February 1969.

I am who I am today because of the Third World Strike at Berkeley in 1969 and the beginning of Ethnic Studies at CAL.

Who am I? I consider myself a person who stands up for the underdog and for what I think is unjust. I am a nationalist: that is, I am so proud of being Mexican (Mexicans are known for their national patriotism). As a Mexican born in the United States, a Chicana, there is so much history, culture, art, music, and food to back me up.

I was born and raised in Salinas, California. My mom's efforts and hard work got me and my five siblings into Catholic school. The curriculum was straightforward, Eurocentric, filled with multiplication drills and religion as a daily class. My father provided the roof over our heads. We grew up in a pretty secure environment, where kids were out playing kick-the-can and hide-and-go-seek with other neighborhood kids until 9 o'clock at night. Knowing that I went to Catholic school for 12 years and that I was from the rural, farmworkers area of Salinas, you can probably guess that I grew up pretty conservatively political with a hint of social justice consciousness. At the same time, I recall that Mexican was considered a dirty word in the '50s and '60s. so when I would go to the local beauty college to get a permanent for my straight hair and was asked if I was Spanish, I would always nod my head solemnly and affirmatively.

After attending Hartnell Community College in Salinas, I was accepted into UC Berkeley. For financial reasons, I moved into Stebbins Hall, a co-op on the north side of campus. I dutifully attended classes and went to the library in the evenings. But one fall evening, I saw students protesting and hanging outside the second-floor windows of Moses Hall in support of Eldridge Cleaver, a Black Panther Party member. That was my introduction to student politics!

I then met Ysidro Macias, one of the Chicano leaders on campus. He invited me to attend a MASC (Mexican American Student Confederation) meeting in Dwinelle Hall where there was a discussion about a possible strike on campus by students of color who wanted to create an Ethnic Studies College on campus. When the vote was taken, it was affirmative. We would join the other students – Asian, Black, Native American – in demanding an Ethnic Studies Program and future Third World College.

Why? Other than some Latin American Studies and Spanish classes, it was impossible to find relevant classes. Classes about the experiences of Mexicans in the US were almost non-existent. This was the same for other communities of color. Self-determination became an important concept for us. That is, we wanted to determine our future by taking courses that were meaningful and germane to us; courses that were taught by people who looked like us. We also wanted a voice in decisions impacting students of color.

On January 20, 1969, we went on strike. I was a foot soldier, not a leader. Every morning at 8am, I could be found at the Chicano Art Center, a bungalow on Channing Street just above Telegraph, picking up the mimeographs that we would pass out to fellow students. Then, I would spend part of my day on the picket lines at the corners of Telegraph and Bancroft, Sather Gate, and the north side entrance of the campus at Euclid and Hearst, passing out flyers to students.

There were serpentine marches across campus around noon almost every day. We went all over campus — north, south, east, and west — with a major focus on Sather Hall and Dwinelle. It was a primary place where we would encounter one of two groups of cops. One group was the UC police, and the other was the "Blue Meanies" of Alameda County. Mean and big they were! We would enter Sproul shouting out slogans, "On strike, shut it down!" We entered and exited pretty quickly because UC police had their officers downstairs who handcuffed students and transported them to Santa Rita prison. Once, as we marched past Dwinelle, we ran into a gang of Blue Meanies who lobbed tear gas at us. We ran in the opposite direction.

I remember the time we were protesting in front of Sather Hall. The cops ran, grabbed Ysidro, beat him with billy clubs, and dragged him away. He ended up in the hospital with a concussion. Many other students were also arrested at different times. During our 10-week strike, I would go to the four co-ops on Ridge Road during dinner and address the students about the strike. That gave a shy kid from Salinas an opportunity to practice some courage and public speaking skills.

The strike dragged on for 10 weeks, lasting the whole winter quarter. That was the longest student strike. I never attended classes during the strike but I did take finals to not flunk out of Cal. In the end, Berkeley's faculty Senate voted to establish a department of Ethnic Studies.

The fight for a Third World college would be an ongoing struggle. I took as many classes as I could. It was great. I learned so much about Chicano history, my people and our role in our country's development. It was and still is so empowering. Meanwhile, I was working as a work study student at the Chicano Studies. I was a bibliographer working with another student to research relevant books, purchase old historical books from bookstores throughout the state, and catalog them. That was the beginning of the Chicano Studies library which would eventually merge with the Ethnic Studies Library in 1997. I am really proud of that too.

In retrospect, I realize how quickly I became politicized during the student strike. I moved from a hyphenated Mexican-American, a government approved term, to a word that I fully embraces — Chicana! I was very proud about uniting with other people of color for a common cause. The strike helped provide me with a foundation for who I am politically today. Fifty years ago, I was a Mexican-American who transformed into a Chicana with an additional consciousness of my connection to people of color.

In my continuing long journey, I gave voice to my people's concerns by becoming a teacher and a principal. For 30 years, I worked in public schools in Berkeley, Oakland, and San Francisco. Educating children of color was my mission. Working side by side with the Mexican community in Oakland's Jingle town, we created the first charter school there in 1993. It answered a great need of the parents. Today I am retired, but I continue to serve the community of my grandchildren by being elected to the Board of Education of Albany Unified School District. Here I continue to consciously raise my voice in order to bring marginalized groups of students and their parents to the decision-making table. My participation in the Third World Strike at UC Berkeley prepared me well for this day.

*TWLF/twLF Intergenerational Mixer at Multicultural Community Center. October 6, 2018. Harvey Dong photo.*

# It's the Peoples University

CLEMENTINA DURON

*Remarks at TWLF Exhibit of Doe Library, UC Berkeley on April 24, 2019.*

First, I would like to thank everyone who made this TWLF commemoration symposium happen. So many students and staff have worked really hard to bring together some dynamic speakers, thoughtful and challenging themes, and an impressive exhibit.

But when I think about whom I should specifically name, I hesitate because I realize that today I put people at risk to name them here at the University. After almost 5 decades away from campus with just an occasional visit, it has only been in the last year that I have spent any substantial time on campus. Yet I find that there is a palpable atmosphere here on campus that is oppressive and intimidating for students.

The theme tonight is "Whose University?" I find this so appropriate because you would think that, 50 years after the Third World Student Strike, there would be tangible and significant progress in terms of the number of professors, types of courses, and students of color on campus. That there would be a thriving, meaningful Ethnic Studies/Third World College. But sadly, that is not the case.

Fifty years ago, we fought for what we considered to be our basic right - to see ourselves reflected in the curriculum and in those who taught us. We stood pretty strong for ten weeks as we walked picket lines and passed out literature, marched through the campus, and spoke at rallies, dorms and co-ops.

I think that the continued lessons from the legacy of the TWLF is that every moment -- at every turn -- you must be willing to stand up and fight for what you believe in. Nobody gives up power willingly. Self-determination is as key today as it was 50 years ago. Solidarity is likewise as crucial. We need to find our commonalities and work together because divide and conquer is so easy for the institution.

The Ethnic Studies Library exhibit offers us a reflection of the many years of continued conflict. The newspaper clips and photos, posters and other artifacts tell a story that resonate not only 50 years ago, not only in 1999 with a focus on Ethic Studies, Radical Politics and Beyond the School Industrial Complex, not only in 2010, but also today. Retaliation and oppression are real for current students as they search for critical education, social justice, and change.

The struggle in and of itself is liberating when we fight for our rights to a meaningful education, when we stand with our allies in a similar struggle, and when we recognize that the good fight never ends.

What I take away from this exhibit is that in the on-going struggle for social change, while we recognize that the terms we use to identify ourselves and our experiences change over time, the fundamental issues do not. That is, all people deserve respect and full participation in our institutions.

I understand that there are different offices on campus that address inclusion and diversity. But THIS is a contradiction when Ethnic Studies today is a mere skeleton of how it started off - with a curriculum and faculty that taught our history and motivated us to work in our communities. Over the last 50 years UC has continually marginalized and undermined Ethnic Studies by reducing funds, thereby leading to less faculty and courses, and a determined lack of support for the creation of a Third World College as was intended by the '69 strike.

At the same time, there is a state move underway to make Ethnic Studies mandatory at the high school level. This particularly resonates with me as a former Chicana public school educator. For 30 years, I witnessed our numbers grow until today we represent over 50% of the public school student population in California. But at Cal, Latinos are less than 15% of the students and Chicano/ Latino faculty make up an embarrassing 6%. The other groups of color do poorly as well.

Our goal at Cal should be full representation of all groups minimally at a level of parity to their population. Ethnic Studies/Third World College should be a vital and core component of the University's curriculum and faculty should work in conjunction with the curriculum and the training of high school Ethnic Studies teachers. Furthermore, Berkeley should be moving forward in providing a resilient and expansive Ethnic Studies/Third World College.

Once again, whose University? It's the people's university. And that means all of us. Today in California people of color are the majority. Yet we continue to struggle. Our issues, our faces, our education should be an integral part of the University. That is our challenge and that is why we are here tonight. We need to continue to stand up and have our voices heard. Yes, we can! Si Se Puede!

*Second from right: Clementina Duron with TWLF veterans at Multicultural Community Center. October 6, 2018. Harvey Dong photo.*

# 50 Years Later: The Struggle for Social Justice Continues

*FLOYD HUEN*

*Left: Floyd Huen. Right: strikers including Jean Quan. 1969. Doug Wachter photo.*

In October 2018, 11 Jewish people were killed in their synagogue at Pittsburg, Pennsylvania. Numerous leaders of the Democratic Party were mailed pipe bombs from a white nationalist fanatic. Hate crimes have increased by 57% over the last year. Our country is in a moral crisis. The question last November 6 was, what type of country do we want? The victory by 40 seats of Democrats was at least a temporary rebuke to Trump.

What we do in the next few years will determine the answer to the question posed on November 6. In the Chinese community, there is a resurgence of interest in our history and cultural contributions capped by the 15th Golden Spike ceremonies in Utah. This past year, Ric Burns co-directed an excellent two-hour PBS edition of the Chinese Exclusion Act, making the detailed history available to millions of Americans and particularly Asian Americans.

As we approach the celebration of 50 years since the founding of the Ethnic Studies department at the University of California, Berkeley and San Francisco State University, we need to take stock of how far we have come. There has been a lot of progress; most major universities offer some Ethnic Studies while here in California, legislation has mandated school districts to teach Ethnic Studies starting in 2019.

We just put down a marker at 2005 Hearst Str, Berkeley to show how and when the Asian American Political Alliance (AAPA) was founded. I invite all to witness it. It was the birthplace of the Asian American movement.

Although the founding of our two programs were intertwined, the Third World College at SFSU thrives while the Ethnic Studies program at UCB stagnates and requires revitalization.

Many students at UCB asked us to help reform AAPA. We have. Only a student led movement with the support of communities can affect change on the campuses. However, political forces need to be brought to bear as well as the promise of self-determination demanded by the TWLF can be realized: student initiative, community oriented, service learning.

Here in Oakland, my wife Jean Quan became the very first Chinese American mayor of a major American city. In San Francisco, Eric Mar joined the Board of Supervisors and Ed Lee was elected mayor. Now, Eric's brother, Gordon, is elected in the Chinese plurality Sunset district. His labor orientation will jive well with the working-class base in that district. It is high time for our elected officials to take stock of the past 50 years as well.

Once again, just like in the 1960s, California is called on to lead the way. All of the above represent great opportunities, but the real question is about leadership. I feel as though we need to work with the UCB students to reestablish AAPA in the community as well as to take on big issues emerging. In a multicultural America, how do we find redress from the years of Chinese exclusion and elimination at Chinatowns all over California?

Eleven Jewish community members shot dead in Pittsburg is the modern day version of the burnings of our Chinatowns. The actions addressed in Pittsburg going forward mirror the ones needed to address the Exclusion Act and anti-Chinese violence. That is the task of our Asian American Studies program, especially in California.

*TWLF march through Sproul Plaza. Winter 1969. Doug Wachter photo.*

# Without Hesitation, I Voted to Strike

FRANCISCO HERNANDEZ

*Serpentine line marches through campus. Winter 1969. Doug Wachter photo.*

As I walked into a meeting with the Chicano students early in 1969, I had just started my second quarter at Berkeley. During the first quarter, I had heard of students striking at San Francisco State University demanding the creation of an ethnic studies college. I had not followed the strike other than what came across on the KQED news hour. I had been involved with the activist students at Berkeley but only on the periphery.

That night the debate was difficult and tense. We were asked to consider joining a student strike of our own in cooperation and collaboration with the other ethnic minority student groups on the Berkeley campus. Some argued to strike, but others argued to refrain from joining. Should we strike in demand of an ethnic studies college or should we wait and demand our own department of Chicano studies? Will the other student groups join us in solidarity or use us for their own ends? Should we sacrifice our own individual goals for a dramatic change within the university or should we not jeopardize our education that we planned to use in serving our community? What if the strike failed, or we were arrested and dismissed from campus? We had fought so hard to get into

Berkeley. Many had sacrificed for us to get into college. Why would we now undo all those sacrifices? Why would we take such a risk?

As the arguments became more heated, those in the meeting became more divided. Those divisions reflected the existing differences in our struggle's history but would also foretell more permanent schisms within the larger Chicano student movement. The debates of that night would reverberate throughout my entire higher education career.

When it came time to vote, I voted to strike. As the words came out of my mouth, I wondered what my parents would say, or more importantly, what did I just do to my future?

I spent the night before the strike in the Chicano Center 'guarding' the picket signs we had just made. I thought much and slept little because you can't get comfortable on top of a hundred picket signs.

I recall walking the picket line, marching through the campus, and yelling at other students to join the strike. I spoke at evening meetings to explain the strike to other students and listened to continuous arguments about upcoming events. I remember the smell of tear gas, the reflection of my face in the masks of county sheriffs, and the highway patrol officers who gathered to control the strikers. The sounds of people running from that tear gas and those officers. I also remember the thrill of watching so many people of so many different ethnic backgrounds gathered together on the picket lines, in meetings, at parties, and gatherings. In those spaces, I saw unapologetic and fearless expressions of our own ethnic cultures.

With picket lines, chants, cheers of support, and jeers of disdain from fellow students, each day seemed like the day. Picketing would result in marches that were followed with disruption of campus activities, the damaging of campus facilities, followed by police actions against the student strikers. Sometimes that included attempts to break the picket lines or stop the marches with swinging batons mixed with launching tear gas at us as we fled across the campus. I also remember the fear when running away from the police, especially when they were in the chase with batons. The strike leaders were always targeted through the use of photos taken from rooftops and informants who attended strike information gatherings. Because I was not a strike leader I was fortunate to be able to escape the police actions with only the burning sensation of tear gas and a few blows from a baton while running away across Sproul Plaza.

I remember large rallies and the presence of the National Guard. I wondered just what we had done or what did we represent that merited the presence of so many police and so many weapons including guns. It came to me that we were asking for an opportunity to sit in a classroom and speak about and learn about our own culture; and the response was young men trained for war to make sure that those classroom experiences would not occur. The semester before I had attended thrice-weekly lectures about US history and there had been no one there to stop those classes.

The faculties in charge of my coursework were all sympathetic to the strike demands and made accommodations for me to complete my coursework while on strike. Additional support came from sympathetic administrators, other student groups, political organizations and most importantly, community organizations.

The TWLF strike was a life altering experience because for a few weeks I experienced what it was like to join in a critical and common goal with others and to become a part of history rather than just studying history. I learned that this was a community of students struggling to have their voices heard. I learned about how others who came before me truly sacrificed their lives and well being as witnessed by the farmworker's grape strike. I learned about the cultural mores and rich histories of my fellow students. I learned the importance of organization, motivation, goal setting, and a steadfastness to achieve important goals. I learned how to be one of many.

On another night in the same classroom where we had voted to strike we voted to accept the university's offer and settle the strike. We did not achieve our goal nor has that goal been achieved in the intervening 50 years. There is no happy ending to this short interval of the struggles of our student community. I only take solace in the personal knowledge that many students from our communities have taken great benefit and were given needed support through the work of the Chicano Studies program that resulted from the strike.

Fifty years later I can say without hesitation that if I had to do it all over again I would again vote to be a part of the TWLF strike of 1969.

*Celebratory event for TWLF/twLF 50th, Berkeley, California. April 2019. Harvey Dong photo.*

# Lessons Learned from the Third World Strike

*LILLIAN FABROS*

*Lillian Fabros, daughter of a Filipino American farmworker, visits artichoke fields. Castroville, Ca 1976. Liz Del Sol photo.*

At the 40th anniversary of the Third World Strike, I gave a speech on "Life Lessons Learned from the Third World Strike *(that I didn't realize until much later).*" These were basic principles of community involvement and radical organizing that have held fast during and since the strike. I want to encourage the next generation of Asian American activists, especially because of the current political situation and racist attitudes in the U.S. But I realize that in order to do so, we need to remember and write the history of the struggle for recognition of the contributions Asian Americans have made to this country.

Lesson 1: Build Coalitions Before You Need Them. It is essential to build coalitions with like-minded groups before you need their help. Otherwise, it comes off as opportunistic, and questions arise whether you will reciprocate in supporting them after they've supported you. AAPA started the basis for coalition building among the different Asian groups. In months and years to come, Filipino Americans would come to support the laws against Japanese

American, and also the children of Japanese American farm owners would support the Pilipino farm workers striking for fair wages. Likewise, members of AAPA began supporting and building relationships with other minority groups. By the time the Third World Strike began in January 1969, AAPA had strong relationships with the Black, Chicano, and other groups. If these connections had not taken place before the Third World strike, it is doubtful that such a strong alliance based on mutual respect and trust would have been forged.

<u>Lesson 2: Race Matters</u>. It was important then – and it still is important now – race absolutely matters. Even 50 years ago, Asians were touted as the "model minority." Chinese and Japanese were seen as having overcome racism. As a result, it was at times difficult to convince other Asians and Asian Americans to support the Third World strike, as many did not feel they were being discriminated against and there was no need for a Third World College. Ironically, many of these same Asians did not know that Japanese Americans had been forced into camps during WWII. No race has "made it" until all races have made it.

<u>Lesson 3: Class Matters – Never Forget Class Background.</u> It is very difficult for individuals from privileged backgrounds, including those of color, to truly understand the barriers faced by people of lesser economic means. Berkeley students could aspire to better economic status or even to the continuance of their upper-class status and feel they had nothing to gain by supporting the strike. Some of the worst oppressors of Asians have been our own people.

<u>Lesson 4: Women Hold Up Half the Sky.</u> Asian women accounted to at least half, if not more, of the Asian students actively involved in supporting the Third World strike. This was in sharp contrast to the Black and Chicano student groups, where women were far fewer. Asian women's dedication has proven to be true in multiple endeavors afterwards, as advocates for civil rights, directors of service organizations, etc.

<u>Lesson 5: Organize, Organize, Organize</u>. It is difficult for individuals on their own to bring about change. And you can never stop organizing because gains can disappear, momentum can be lost, as we have seen lately. Organizing means working with a broad spectrum of supporters to build a multitude of strategies and programs.

<u>Lesson 6: The Journey is as Important as the Goal.</u> It is arguable that because the strike ultimately ended in a moratorium, there was no victory for Third World students. For me the victory was the jumpstarting of Asian American

activism over the past decades. I have lifelong friends, men and women who I marched with in picket lines back in Berkeley. These friends have gone on to work against racism in different ways over the past five decades. The strike coalesced a longing for justice that expressed itself in multiple personal and professional endeavors.

Lesson 7: Find the Goal You are Passionate About. In the 70s there was a push for working in the community, even to the point of working with laborers, troubled youth, disenfranchised folks, and the "lumpen proletariat." I recall vividly instances of well-meaning activists awkwardly and probably ineffectively trying to relate to youth, awkwardly trying to organize or unionize workers, etc. Yet despite this philosophical or political mantra, many did not remain in the community to continue their initial work. This reminded me of what happened in the fields in the Salinas Valley. We need a broad range of skills for people such as writers, researchers, doctors, union organizers because they will remain committed to helping the communities when they remember their roots. There are different paths to furthering justice.

*Strike activities at UC Berkeley. Lillian Fabros is second from right. Winter 1969. Doug Wachter photo.*

# Video Clip (Poet as Young Revolutionary, Berkeley 1969)

JEFFREY THOMAS LEONG

TWLF 50th, Jeffrey Leong reads original TWLF demands for a Third World College. January 22, 2019, Mario Savio (Sproul) Steps, UC Berkeley. Harvey Dong photo.

Before cameras at the news conference, he so precise and bold,
exacting, yet more heated than I recall.
What felt was suffered there?

Aunt Edna, cranium-cracked in the Model-T's splash,
struck by a white Delta rancher, *but no justice*,
Chinese couldn't testify in court.

Or his *parents' lowered gaze* as that realtor wouldn't show
a house in El Cerrito,
amidst the East Bay's blonde hills?

Here, a 19-year-old in profile, not one crease nor pimple,

no masking gray, receding temples,
but his angry lips amply full (our one faithful constant).

In Eshlemann's chambers before a mic, youth flares
in Don Davis's haloed afro,
Ysidro's shaky smoke-spiraling hand,

and this Chinese American teen chosen to enunciate the *5 demands*
for Third World student strike, a shout out
orchestrated by politicos

(his leader too levied with the FBI to go, but that
secret as yet unrevealed).
So just now, his tortoise-shell rims adhesive-taped,

curly locks still jet-black, and clad in a camouflaged
poncho like a hunter ex-hippie,
he begins to articulate,

to say what hadn't been uttered before
but what's to be declared over and
once again.

What news yet gathers upon this mini-screen?
A boy is but once,
and though revolutions may play and flip,

change so framed, once affixed,
holds the essence in
a video clip.

*18 March 2013 (2nd version; (Revised - 4 January 2019)*

*TWLF Medic Team. Winter 1969. Doug Wachter photo.*

*Strikers march through Lower Sproul Plaza. Winter 1969. Doug Wachter photo.*

*Supporter with sign: "On Strike. Support TWLF." Winter 1969. Doug Wachter photo.*

*Student picketing in front of campus cops. Winter 1969. Doug Wachter photo.*

# Chapter Three:
# **New Generations**

# Memories of TWLF

*RICKEY VINCENT*

Left: Rickey Vincent photo. Right: Daily Cal reports passage of American Cultures requirement. February 1987.

Growing up in Berkeley in the 70s, in an activist household, the TWLF was a backdrop to what we believed was possible. The "Third World Strike" at SF State (and later at Cal) gave my generation hope that a multiracial coalition, led by black & brown activists, could challenge the power of The State and not only survive but change the game. The mainstream social change narrative of that era lauds the 1964 "Free Speech Movement" as the iconic social movement breakthrough at Berkeley, but that was to me a distant backdrop to the changes that were closer to home. Ethnic Studies was how we lived. I was proud to graduate with an Ethnic Studies degree in 1987, and proud to walk in 2007 with a Doctorate in Ethnic Studies from the same stage at UC Berkeley.

As a youth, I watched my mother, Toni Vincent, organize with the Third World Women's Alliance in the 1970s. We organized events, participated in rallies, and showed solidarity with struggles all across the region and around the world. Multi-racial revolutionary solidarity made sense to me. My mother's organization the TWWA was originally black led, the Black Women's Alliance, and adapted to include Puerto Rican women in the Northeast where it began, and then all women of color when it expanded to the West Coast. Much like the TWLF evolved from the work of a black organization the *Black Liberation Front*, the starting point was from grassroots black organizing.

As an undergrad in the 1980s, and later as a grad student in the early 2000s, we framed the TWLF with a bit of romance, as a time when courageous student-activists challenged the status quo and created a new one. At the time, I was like many people who had few firm details about what exactly happened and how it went down. But I knew it went a bit deeper.

Growing up in Berkeley I remember the National Guard troops standing outside my elementary school, and the chaotic riots on Telegraph Avenue that my father and brother found themselves embroiled in. Was it an anti-war protest? A People's Park riot? An Ethnic Studies march? It was all one big revolutionary moment for me. So, I had an inherent understanding that it took monumental lifting to get Ethnic Studies programs off the ground, and that reconstructing the story would not be simple. What I initially found would be piecemeal, and the information occasionally unsavory and violent. I was not surprised when I came across former activists of the TWLF (SF and Berkeley) movements, who instead of beaming with pride, and joy of retelling a narrative, sometimes spoke in guarded terms, with a reluctance to full disclosure that was disconcerting, but not surprising.

I had a similar experience working with the Anti-Apartheid protests at UC Berkeley in the 1980s. There were so many moving parts and varied accounts of that massive (and successful) effort to change the practices (or at least earn a promise of change in practices) of the UC system's financial dealings, that there was little consensus of what was the trigger point for our victory, and how it came about. Was it the months long Sproul Plaza (Biko Plaza) protests? The "Shanty Towns" built on campus? The broad organizing between students, staff, community, & labor movements? Was it the shrewd backroom negotiations? Was it the escalating events in South Africa? It all came together in terms of winning *Divestment* in 1987, but I don't remember having a party to celebrate. (A newly freed Nelson Mandela did come to the Oakland Coliseum in 1990, and thanked the UC Students then.) In a process that is eerie similar, both the Divestment and Third World College struggles created so much enmity among the participants, that no one effectively is in place to be a central voice, an authority on either subject.

Yet the evidence is there, the proof is in the results. Mandela was freed, and elected President of South Africa, and Ethnic Studies programs are everywhere. The TWLF may be one of the most successful and long-lasting movements of my lifetime, even if there is precious little popular narrative history of their victory on the ground level. Maybe the actions of the members of the TWLF are not listed prominently in any handbook for community organizing, but remembering their work is our duty and our calling.

There is another issue complicating the matter of the TWLF legacy, because the opponents of Ethnic Studies have been diligently studying what happened and working on how to devise means to contain & eliminate the progress made back then. When I look at how locked in & intransigent the bureaucracy is in colleges around the Bay Area, and how many 'liberal' and outwardly well-meaning administrators claim "the rules say we cannot expand your program," "or" the rules say we cannot add a full-time professor here," or "we cannot make a part-timer a full timer, because of the process . . ." they can conveniently hide behind 'the process.' What became clear to me was that the TWLF quite strategically *blew up* the process. In the fluid aftermath, people were able to create and innovate in African American Studies, Ethnic Studies, Diversity Studies and all kinds of relevant fields dedicated to exploring the narratives of underrepresented people in America. But it appears that the ubiquity of 'the process' has returned, with a smothering bureaucracy, that like oozing amber has been coating these programs and fossilizing them in an image frozen in time, and in some cases disintegrating them.

Is a militant-led student movement the answer today? The footage of the chaos on the SF State campus is still mystifying, 50 years later. How did it come to that? Was it by design? Labor activists might say that is what is to be expected in a "work stoppage" of that kind. There were other movements on the ground at the time (anti-Vietnam War, desegregation protests) that also led to state sponsored violence. But in retrospect, how can street protests effectively disentangle the web of control exerted on working class people desiring an education in the 2020s?

The SF State student strike involved everyone from the moneyed power brokers allied with city government, to their police operatives, to campus staff & faculty, to administrators and bureaucrats, to community supporters, to student activists on the right and the left going at one another. With so much going on, to get some change going, someone had to be pushing hard. A number of the original Black Liberation Front activists were members or allies of the Black Panther Party. The Party had a far-reaching community organization, and *Self-Determination* was their mantra. Rank-and-file Panthers did the footwork, legwork, paperwork, and whatever work was necessary. It is not mentioned very often, but Point Number Five of the BPP Ten Point Program was: *"We want education for our people that exposes the true nature of this decadent American society. We want education that teaches us our true history and our role in the present-day society."* An argument can be made that on this point (along with the Oakland Community School and other efforts) the SF State Student Strike can be seen as one of the crowning achievements of the Black Panthers' many contributions to social change.

I know when I teach classes on the Black Panther Party and Popular Culture, I tell my students the first day and every day "you don't have to agree with what these people said or did, but you should be familiar with what was accomplished and the legacy of their efforts." I think the next generation should move past looking for that 'warm & fuzzy' Civil Rights Movement version of the TWLF and be prepared to look soberly at a time & place where some actions appeared indefensible, and moderates and radicals swam in the same choppy waters. It took a broad swath of the community to affect a sustainable institutional change, and these lessons should be taught with a lively transparency, so the legacy of the work and the institutions that were forged, can be built upon and maintained for generations to come.

## The Anti-Apartheid in South Africa Movement

*In 1987, UC Berkeley student protest pressure succeeded in the divestment of UC investments in South Africa. In 1989, the momentum from the movement laid the foundation for the establishment of the American Cultures requirement at UC Berkeley. Rickey Vincent Photo.*

*Professors Barbara Christian (African American Studies) and Carlos Munoz, Jr participate at rally demanding that UC divest investments in apartheid South Africa. Photo: Barbara Christian Conference Room, Barrows Hall, UC Berkeley.*

# The TWLF Legacy in Immigrant and Refugee Struggles Today

LOAN DAO

*DACA activist and Professor Loan Dao.*

Over the past two decades, Asian American Pacific Islanders (AAPI) have had an increasing presence in the immigrant rights movement. The politics of representation and global solidarity have never been more pertinent to the struggle for human rights. In the current political climate, there has been a growing discrepancy between the dominant rhetoric to delineate "good" and "bad" immigrants and the actuality of sweeping immigrant enforcement in the realms of policy changes, deterrence, arrests, incarceration, and deportation.

Since 2016, even AAPIs who have aligned themselves with the "deservedness" discourse have witnessed increasing draconian policies creating blanket restrictions for Asian immigrants and refugees who enter the U.S. and those already in the country.

In the past two years, the quota for refugees has dramatically decreased. Moreover, the deportation of refugees in the U.S. since the American War in Southeast Asia has also accelerated and expanded in size and scope. There are also new economic requirements and higher standards of professional and educational attainment for people applying for visas from the global south, while the backlog for visas and asylum applications have increased. These geographic and class-based restrictions have resulted in growing numbers of AAPIs living in the U.S. unauthorized and vulnerable to exploitation. Asian and Pacific Islander immigrants constitute the fastest growing undocumented racial group in the country. However, the national discourse on immigration has continued to focus on the Southern border, demonizing refugees, asylum seekers and economic immigrants fleeing from persecution or economic deprivation. Simultaneously, the construction of the Pacific as an "enemy of the state" that is embodies in China and North Korea renders AAPIs in the U.S. vulnerable to anti-immigrant sentiments and racist attitudes pervasive throughout this country's history.

The fight for immigrant rights today extends the legacy of the AAPI's movement in three ways. The movement reclaims the role as historical contributors and members of the nation-state rather than the "perpetual foreigner" stereotype. Activists tie the history of U.S. imperialism in Asia to the push and pull factors. Push factors that force people off their homelands include war, persecution, economic displacement, and extreme poverty. Pull factors attract migrants to the U.S. through labor recruitment by American-based employers, post-war family unification and the exportation of the "American Dream" into the global consumer market.

The framing of the fight for immigrants and refugees to stay thus holds the U.S. accountable for the forces of migration that result in their resettlement in the first place. By making this claim, AAPI in the immigrant rights movement position themselves as seeking justice and accountability of American foreign policy. It shifts the discourse to an open-door immigration policy that corrects past incursions into the Asia Pacific rather than "asking permission" to stay a charitable gift bestowed upon needy immigrants by the generous benefactor, the U.S.

AAPI progressives' positionality on immigrant rights today directly addresses the historical and contemporary racism embedded in American immigration policy while avoiding racial exceptionalism. This generation of activists in the progressive immigrant rights movement have clearly articulated a solidarity to immigrants from the global south are racialized as people of color upon migration into the U.S.

Their solidarity as immigrants and refugees of color take on the legacy of the Third World Liberation Front (TWLF) in their recognition of the geopolitics between the countries of origin and U.S. economic and political imperialist missions in these countries. Their narrative framework rejects the notion of the model minority myth that some Asian Americans adhered to in the 1980s-early 2000s to claim a racial exceptionalism as justification for ethnic or country-specific legislation.

The contemporary movement for immigrant rights among AAPI progressives has expanded into a transnational movement against deportation. While the emergence of TWLF claimed solidarity with international liberation struggles, the evolution of the movement has often been characterized as becoming more concerned with the claims-making and assimilationist tendencies domestically. Today's movement not only understands the ways in which imperialist tendencies have historically shaped migration, but it also recognizes the movement of global capital and surplus labor as causes of deportation – as the byproduct of late capitalism that discards excess, and possibly politically dangerous, "lumpen proletariat" of society. The response, often communicated through the emotional stories of family separation, has been to build transnational solidarity with people who have been deported, from refugee deportees in Cambodia to undocumented adoptees to those who were deported as absconders overstaying their visas. Technological advancements that allow better communication channels between deportees and their families, friends, and movement organizations have completely shifted campaign strategies over the last fifteen years. The goals for international solidarity look at injustice through a neo-colonial relationship with the U.S., and the targets and pressure points for campaigns are now multifaceted. Campaigns target the U.S., receiving countries, and the United Nations to intervene on inhumane detention conditions as well as potential violations to international law rather than just domestic immigration laws and policies. This generation is laying the foundation for a renewed international solidarity movement through the lens of the rights of immigrants and refugees.

At this critical juncture in history, this generation of AAPI immigrant rights activists are reshaping the ways in which we understand immigrant rights within and beyond our borders. Through its connection between the prison pipeline to immigration detention and removal, and its rejection of the model minority as a justification for racial exceptionalism compared to other racialized immigrants, activists are creating a foundation for an international social movement to challenge U.S. foreign policy and hegemony through an immigrant rights framework. However, the movement still has challenges ahead. They still must articulate a cohesive national position on how to demand their right to stay in this country while recognizing the history of stolen land and how Asian Americans participate in settler-colonialism of stolen indigenous lands. They must be careful not to uphold and rely on the legal system, whether domestic or international, to justify and define their human rights; rather, how might they understand human rights as extra-legal and inalienable? Like generations before them, these activists continue to battle internal biases and hierarchies of ethnicity, class, citizenship, gender, sexuality, and colorism within the movement. In the end, when making the decisions on immigration policy, will the people who have most to lose be at the decision-making table? Will their voices and experiences be represented? If not, who is sacrificed when negotiating immigration policy? Today, politicians argue that immigration reform must be "reasonable," or in other words, it cannot be completely inclusive and must include robust funding for enforcement. This generation is beginning to ask, "Can we have immigration reform without more enforcement? Can we Abolish ICE?" AAPI leaders have an opportunity to envision a future for immigrant rights that is "unrealistic." And that is what this moment demands.

# The 1999 twLF Hunger Strike

ROBERTO HERNANDEZ

*Statement read on behalf of Roberto Gonzalez at the 50th TWLF Commemoration rally at UC Berkeley on January 22, 2019.*

Left: 50th Celebration Banner from APASD. January 22, 2020. Right: Roberto Hernandez at Multicultural Community Center. October 6, 2018. Harvey Dong photo.

Good afternoon. I send you greetings on behalf of those of us in 1999, who in the face of budget cuts that sought to starve out our department of ethnic studies through attrition and retirements, found it necessary to reactivate the spirit of those who came before us in 1969 and take on the name once again of the Third World Liberation Front. We did so not out of uninformed and romantic nostalgia, but rather out of the necessity to invoke a resistant spirit that would recognize that at the center of any struggle, it is also the inherent right to know ourselves, to produce and circulate relevant knowledge, accurate knowledge and narratives that work in the service of the people. It was a discussion that we did not take lightly. We did so only after hours and hours of meeting and deliberation.

We did so after a gathering both meant to honor the 30th anniversary of the 1969 TWLF strike and meant as a strategy session to imagine and build a better future for all of us. Only after having been in conversation with our elders, with community members, with faculty, and with each other did we come to the decision that we too had to pick up that mantle and wave the banner of TWLF. We did so because we recognized that this university, whose motto is "let there be light", well over 130 years since its founding remained in the dark when it came to truly valuing not just knowledge *about* communities of color, but more importantly our own ability to engage in critical thought and action for the betterment all lower communities. It became very evident to us that the university, despite its claim to the pursuit of knowledge, instead remained willfully ignorant about the realities of communities of color. Moreover, it was in the university's interest, and indeed remains so, to rely on students coming and going, graduating every few years, and severing the ties of institutional memory from one generation to the next.

So, we said: YA BASTA! ENOUGH!!

On April 11 of 1999, following the gathering for the 30th anniversary, we made a decision that we would take Barrows Hall. This would initiate a month-long campaign of actions, marches, and takeovers that culminated in the even more difficult decision of going on a hunger strike. Ultimately, six of our relatives, our comrades, went on an indefinite hunger strike that lasted eight days before the university, not so much came to its senses, but rather was forced into action by the collective power of the intergenerational organizing by students and community, with faculty also realizing that our department's future laid in the hands of collective action.

While we were ultimately successful, the resulting May 7th Agreement is something that the university has never fully fulfilled. As we remember to be the spirit of those initial relatives that took on the name Third World Liberation Front in 1969 on the occasion of the 50th anniversary, those who are here with us today still putting themselves on the line with us, and those also who have passed away or are too ill to join us, let us remember also that the struggle is far from over. It took us over 500 to get to the mess we are in and it will take us many more to build a better world, a decolonial horizon where an education is about bringing forth the creative energies of life itself and honoring the spirits of our ancestors and the land itself, and not for the production and legitimation of machineries of war and destruction as has become part of the practices of the westernized universities. And as a decolonial *horizon*, let me be clear too, that this means that our continued struggle is not about a destination or endpoint, one where we can then rest while empire seeks to kill and destroy, but a reminder to continue struggle.

As Eduardo Galeano reminds us: of what good is whole is a horizon if one can never reach it? It is meant to keep us walking, to keep us constantly vigilant of the work it entails for building better futures.

The struggle continues! The struggle continues! The struggle continues! The struggle continues! Que viva el TWLF! Viva!!

# African American Studies and the TWLF Strike

ULA TAYLOR

Remarks on TWLF Exhibit Reception at Doe Library, UC Berkeley on April 24, 2019.

Left: Ula Taylor, Professor of African American Studies, UC Berkeley. Right: Ethnic Studies Library TWLF Archival Exhibit Announcement. 2019.

What a wonderful evening to jump start a conversation about the TWLF. This afternoon I had the opportunity to walk through this exhibit, reading statements produced at the time of this explosive moment.

The flier that really caught my eye was "What do you people want?" It has the letters TWLF with stereotypical, sketched, images. Above the letter T is an African American eating a watermelon, a Latino in a sombrero is above the letter W, an Asian person with slanted eyes and a rice field triangle hat is above the L, and a Native American in traditional garb is above the F. Below the four depicted stereotypes is a sketch of then Chancellor Heynes with the question, "What do you people want?"

This question has an echo. That is, there is no point in the history of the United States when white supremacists have not posed this question to people of color. After the passage of the 13th Amendment which removed legal slavery, with the exception for a punishment of a crime, white supremacist asked, what more does the Negro want? After the passage of the 1964 Civil Rights Act and the 1965 Voting Rights Acts, white supremacist asked, what more does the Negro want? The list can go on and on but in the end, we all want to be treated as valued human beings. All of us have histories and cultures that bring value to this world. And here, at CAL, in 1969, students wanted their history and cultural to be recognized in the academy.

When looking at the photos, especially those that capture police repression it's hard to separate the past from the present. It's also hard to separate the past from the present when we look at the African American student population at CAL. The numbers of Black students have ebbed and flowed but since the passage of proposition 209 the numbers have never climbed beyond small percentages. I think today the numbers are a little over 3%. And while we have an African American Studies Department and I proudly serve as its Department Chair, too often it's a place of retreat for students who feel alienated and isolated on campus. Imagine in 2019 still being the only Black person in a class at Berkeley. Or, imagine being in a class and when it's time to break up into small groups people gravitate away from you. Or, imagine being in a class and feeling the pressure that your intellectual opinion will be come off as speaking for the entire "race."

The exhibit not only reminds us of change over time, but also, how much has not changed. I think this is why I am a bit numb. Yes, we have an African American Studies department filled with brilliant, passionate professors who have written transformative scholarship. Professors who teach with their heads and their hearts. But how many of you in this large room today have taken a class that is not linked to an American Cultures requirement? How have notions of white supremacy continued to cloud our current student population in their selection of majors and minors?

In the end, however, all of the images remind us of times when people of color collectively fought back against white supremacy and institutionalized racism. How do we reignite the collective in the midst of individualism? For me that is the biggest take away from this powerful exhibit.

Left: AASU/TWLF strikers. Doug Wachter photo. Right: TWLF, UC Berkeley graphic. Winter 1969

# The Future of Ethnic Studies on its 50th Anniversary: Autonomy and Self-Determination Are Missing

*HARVEY DONG*

*Read at Critical Ethnic Studies Conference, Spring 2018*

50th Anniversary TWLF Rally. Students raise concerns about declining campus support for Asian American and Ethnic Studies courses. Mario Savio (Sproul) Steps, UC Berkeley. January 22, 2019. Harvey Dong photo.

Ethnic Studies at Berkeley remains an unfinished struggle that began almost 50 years ago with the TWLF Strike in 1969. Fundamental questions still remain over program autonomy and direction. Autonomy refers to the right to program control based upon the needs of students and their communities. Successive generations of students seeking to resist inequality and oppression continue to look towards Ethnic Studies relevance as they are confronted with white supremacy, nativism and racism. But student of color actions are often viewed by the campus administration as impatience, unrealistic and harmful to the academic environment.

It can be unequivocally stated that Ethnic Studies exists because of the solidarity and struggle of students supported by faculty and community. The issues of autonomy and self-determination have been at the heart of Ethnic

Studies' protracted 50-year history. Throughout the history of Ethnic Studies and at every level of historical development, administration responses have been enacted to weaken autonomy. Likewise, it is important for every generation of students and entering faculty to understand that student involvement and community engagement have been the lifeblood of the department.

Beginning in 1969, the university administration's denial of program autonomy for the African American Studies proposal led the Afro-American Students Union (AASU) to propose the idea of a TWLF coalition and strike to the Chicano, Asian American, Native American, and Mexican American student groups. Those organizations were also engaging in similar talks with the administration to develop their own programs. Therefore, they were willing to join in coalition because they too had anticipated deadlock negotiations with the administration. They held common cause with the AASU over the issue of autonomy and saw the necessity for a student strike in the establishment of a Third World College.

After the strike, the interim Department of Ethnic Studies began discussing how to transition into its own college. However, it found itself in a continuous struggle with administrative pressures that eventually ended their pursuit towards an establishment of a college. Firstly, African American Studies departed from Ethnic Studies and into the College of Letters of Science (L&S) as its own department. Secondly, the departure of African American Studies in 1974 placed Ethnic Studies into an existential crisis. To fill the void from the departure, Ethnic Studies created a Comparative Ethnic Studies major, transferring and reallocating remaining resources from the Asian American, Chicano and Native American Studies major programs. In turn, the FTE funds from community-based programs were depleted. Nonetheless, despite the lack of funding support, Ethnic Studies still grew into a recognized academic leader in the studies of race and ethnicity.

20 years later, Ethnic Studies followed African American Studies into L&S to become a department with the hopes that there would be more resources, funding and support. The resources did not appear, and the department waned from benign neglect under L&S. Instead of being placed in a more stable position, Ethnic Studies was severely cut back — retired professors were not being replaced and the budget, staff and courses suffered severe funding cuts.

It was only through the efforts of the 1999 twLF student coalition that Ethnic Studies was saved with a short reprieve. Their efforts won 8 faculty FTE positions, the establishment of the Center for Race & Gender, funding for student recruitment and retention programs, the opening of the Multicultural

Community Center, and a mural in Barrows Hall in commemoration of the struggle for Ethnic Studies. The 1999 twLF student efforts regained lost ground and revitalized Ethnic Studies. Faculty support for this was critical. It included vocal support from Ethnic Studies and African American Studies faculty, as well as widespread community support during the several weeks of a hunger strike, rallies and police arrests.

Today, it is still an unfinished struggle: a departure from the original idea of a full college with developed departments, community-based programs, and all with student and community advisory input. Budget cuts have whittled away department and program funding. We are managed as a cluster by L&S but there is no decision input from the below. Instead of more courses, there are less. In comparing the total numbers of Asian American Studies courses offered in 1970 with the numbers offered in Spring 2018, there remains ironically the same number offered: 11. There were 11 instructors listed to teach Asian (American) Studies in 1970 and 11 listed today teaching Asian American & Asian Diaspora Studies (AAADS). A similar situation exists in the other programs.

The idea of a college is not a pipedream. It exists at San Francisco State University. Ethnic Studies exists there not as a department but as a college with its own deans. Their existence was also the result of struggle and solidarity. In the Spring 2018 semester, course offerings at SFSU are much higher than UCB's offerings. Asian American Studies at SFSU has 28 classes, Latino/a American Studies holds 31 classes, American Indian Studies has 13 classes, Race and Resistance Studies has 23 classes, and Africana Studies has 23 classes. In addition, Arab and Muslim Ethnicities and Diaspora Studies at SFSU was recently established. In comparison, the Ethnic Studies programs at UC Berkeley have been pared down disgracefully less than SFSU's Spring 2018 offerings. Full departments exist at SFSU with departmental control over each curriculum. The only programs existing in UCB Ethnic Studies are: AAADS, Chicano, Native American, and Comparative Ethnic Studies, and their futures are decided through a departmental executive committee of higher ranked faculty.

It may be difficult to envision the possibilities at UC Berkeley because the box has been so closed over the years. It may be difficult to grasp for faculty because it takes an extraordinary amount of time to be devoted to turn the situation around much less finish personal academic research and teaching responsibilities. The current state of affairs calls for solutions that require dialogue between students, faculty, community representatives, and the university. A dialogue that occurred in 1999 about the possibilities of bringing Ethnic

Studies and African American Studies back into one amalgamation needs to be continued. The two histories and futures are interconnected. Whatever happens in the next 50 years with Ethnic Studies needs to be discussed not in isolation from each other, but through a unified voice and vision for the future. It can be a win-win for the campus, the field of Ethnic Studies, African American Studies, Asian American & Asian Diaspora Studies, Chicana/o & Latina/o Studies, Native American Studies, and the broader community but only if we seriously wish to make it happen.

# What Can Asian American Studies Be?

*ASIAN AMERICAN STUDIES COALITION AT CAL*
*Spring 2018*

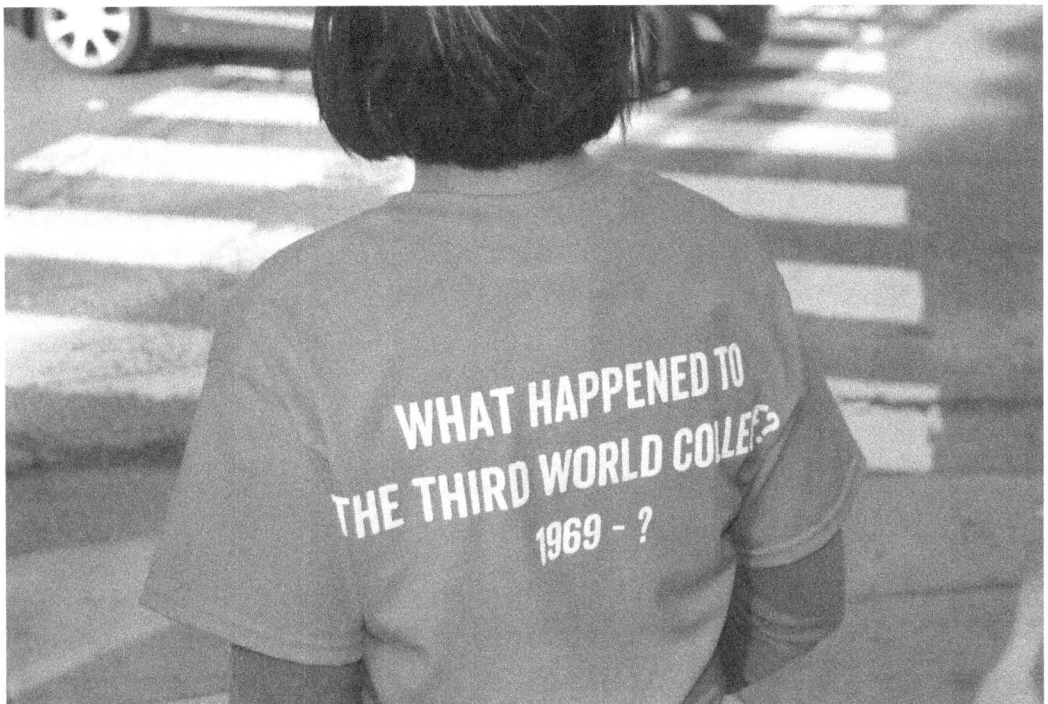

**Intro/Revisiting the Origins of Asian American Studies**

In 1969, inspired by the San Francisco State College Strike and other radical movements of the time, under the banner and unity of the Third World Liberation Front, UC Berkeley students and community came together to demand and create a revolutionary education. Part of this demand was the creation of Asian Studies (now Asian American Studies/Asian American and Asian Diaspora Studies) as part of a greater Third World College, an education that would prioritize the liberation of oppressed and marginalized communities.

Unfortunately, the demand for an autonomous College was never met. Third World Studies - now Ethnic Studies - became a department under the College of Letters and Science, and Asian American Studies became a program under this department. As the decades went on, though there were repeated demands to grow this program and to match the needs of a rapidly changing Asian America, the program and department repeatedly faced cutbacks, ameliorated only by student and community pushback.

## Present

In Spring of 2018, Asian American Studies students came together to discuss the state of the program. Our conversations and thoughts ranged from our love of the field, our dissatisfactions with the course content and facilitation, the lack of community engagement, and our reflections on what Asian American Studies was *supposed* to be. We asked a simple question: what happened?

Thus, the #what happened shirt campaign began with the intention to start conversations about Asian American Studies across campus. We organized internally, from asking faculty to engage with us in our concerns and thoughts to engaging with other students. Some of us created surveys while others held conversations and sessions to evaluate what students at Cal--majors and minors and all --were feeling about the current state of Asian American Studies. Additionally, many beyond our campus also engaged, demonstrating the ongoing pride and hunger for Asian American Studies.

Here is what we have heard and engaged with so far. Listen --

## Student Experiences/Thoughts

We recognize the dissonance between our education and lived experience in Asian American Studies. There is a yearning for content that reflects our communities and our lives. We do not find diversity nor liberation in courses that render South Asian/Southeast Asian/Pacific Islander narratives invisible, ignore the intersectionality of various oppressive systems, and do not acknowledge the possibilities of our liberations being tied to others'.

We want skills, histories, and frameworks that uplift our long-overlooked communities modeled within the curriculum and classroom. As an integral part of our education, we desire to carry the memory of Asian Americans outside of this ivory tower. Currently, students bear the brunt of this labor of teaching and modeling and working while only learning academic theory in a classroom that looks exactly the same as in any other department: hierarchical and removed.

We are frustrated, too, within our own program, with professors that seem disconnected and uninterested in engaging with us as students, unaware or uncaring of the ways in which they also harm us through microaggressions and dismissals. At the same time, we do recognize their difficult position as people subject to the university in ways we as students are not.

We understand that our program is not dying a natural death because of a lack of student interest. It is being starved of resources, of funding, of staff, of opportunities to expand and engage. We are aware, albeit slowly, of the gradual budget cuts that diminish our program, of the gains that have been lost, and of a quickly fading memory as student turnover depletes institutional knowledge.

We see the ways in which the Asian American Studies program, as well as Ethnic Studies, has been cut down by a university that does not - and *can not* - value the education, the power, and the possibilities this field holds.

## Futurity

We are grateful to each other and to our community who have supported us in the past and present. All of the statements are drawn from student efforts at gathering information and engaging with others, from surveys with long responses and individual conversations that we hope to preserve for the future.

Although this statement comes at the end of the year, we, in love, continue to hope and strive for a transformative Asian American Studies, where our practice is as important as our goals and where the ways we interact with each other are also places of unlearning oppressions and trauma. We look forward to continuing our conversations, our efforts at building student and community power, and asking not only, "What happened to Asian American Studies?" but, "What can Asian American Studies *be*?" and "*How do we get there*?"

## Additional References

http://revolution.berkeley.edu/projects/twlf/

*"A Broken Promise 50 Years. Where is Our Third World College?" Sign held at 50th commemoration of TWLF Strike. Left to right: Cynthia Ledesma, Abraham Ramirez and Pablo Gonzalez. November 22, 2019. Harvey Dong photo.*

# #WhatHappened Campaign: The Current & Future State of AAADS

*JACKLIN HA*

*Spring 2019*

"What Happened to Asian American Studies?" T-Shirt Campaign raised student concerns about the future of the program. 2019. Harvey Dong photo.

Our recent #WhatHappened campaign asked the question, "What Happened to Asian American Studies? What Happened to the Third World College? 1969-? Not only does this campaign challenge the intent of the department, but also the internal relations within the department.

This paper aims to explore the establishment of AAADS (Asian American & Asian Diaspora Studies) at UC Berkeley in an attempt to understand what really happened to AAADS following the TWLF strike. Between 2018-9, student opinions have been collected anonymously through a google form with a few of the responses analyzed below.

The survey was sent out to students within and out of the department as well as alumni and community members with a total of 12 respondents. This was a preliminary independent student-run study and there are still many in depth responses to analyze. Of the students who filled out the survey, there was a wide spectrum of majors and minors which included: AAADS, business, cognitive science, history, Japanese, integrative biology, Japanese language and literature, nutritional science, and public health. 75% of the respondents had taken an AAADS course before with ASAMST 20A (Asian American History) as the majority. Two of the respondents who had taken 20A reported that they looked forward to taking more classes and included some possible choices.

A respondent also elaborated further saying that they "really liked ASAMST 20A since it was the first time [they have] ever heard about the hxstory of Pilipinx folx as well as the hxstory of other AAPI folx. [They] never had that kind of exposure back home and so learning about those experiences in ASAMST 20A was very *empowering*. One respondent who had not taken any AAADS courses reported that they "would love to, but there is no room in [their] schedule for non-major classes."

What was interesting was that most of the respondents took courses that are within group 2 (community studies) of AAADS courses, showing an interest this specific group over groups 1 (history) and 3 (cultural studies).

When asked what they would want to get out of the AAADS department or classes within the department, a majority of the respondents mentioned wanting to understand "[their] own culture and position within this country," assuming that they identify as Asian/Asian-American, as well as being able to "learn more about the hxstories of AA/PI communities".

One respondent phrased this eloquently:

*"[I want to] learn more about who I am in America, and gain tools and knowledges to better our communities within the realm of Asian America as well as broader coalition building. I want to be moved by our past and understand where our current issues lie, and the uniqueness of our legacy as Asian Americans. I want to learn a framework for understanding our society that is simultaneously critical and hopeful."*

As for respondents who have not taken an AAADS course, they voiced that they would want to understand the history of Asian American communities beyond what has been taught in US history classes. This is true. Unfortunately, many of our K-12 curriculum do not include American history outside of white American history; especially if students, faculty, and community members had to go on strike in order to secure an ethnic studies department at the collegiate level. Another interesting thought is that within the state of California, at least there is talk of an ethnic studies department, "at the K-12 level, Asian American Studies remains relatively absent, in particular outside of California" (Dhingra and Rodriguez 94).

## Opportunities for Community Engagement

Again, a good number of respondents also mentioned that they wanted "opportunities to get engaged in Asian American organizations/projects in the local community" with "more variety in classes, decals ran by students, career pathways, and field trips".

It seems that, at least so far among this population of respondents, a bridge between what is learned within the classroom and what is brought out to the community is of significance, and isn't that what the department should be preparing the students for?

While respondents acknowledge the department's ability to create a community space with more inter-student interactions and good advising, still, at least 1/3 of the respondents was unsure of what areas the department has been strong in. Admittedly as a double major in AAADS and integrative biology, I have seen and can attest to the smaller community space that is created within AAADS classes of 30-50 versus a science class of 800-1600 students. However, what does it mean for the department if a good number of respondents were unsure or refrained from answering the question of the department's strengths?

Overall, though, many respondents felt that they were content with the student interactions within class, but student engagement outside of the class is low. Does this suggest that community is only created within the learning environment and what is taught about community isn't really brought out to the community space? One respondent laid out:

*"Some classes really shine, whereas others fall short in terms of content diversity and classroom environment. I wish there was more community, more interactions with professors, and I wish professors would encourage our different interactions with community more and regard that as an integral part of our education. I wish there were more classes, and more diversity among the classes—I feel like I rarely learn about South Asians, for example. I am mostly neutral, leaning towards negative for the department—I feel like they are not very transparent with their students, and many professors (though certainly not all) don't seem to care much about the students or even the subject and the field's original vision beyond research and class. The lecturers, for the most part, seem to be more true to the field's vision." ("The Current & Future State of AAADS")*

The thought about more diversity among classes was not an opinion of this respondent alone but of a few others who felt that "only the East Asian side is being represented primarily [and they] hardly ever see the West and South Asian being represented when we speak about Asian communities in general." If we look at the courses listed in the AAADS website, we do see that communities other than East Asia are included in group 1 (history). However, moving into group 2 (community studies), we only see 2 of 10 courses that are specific to an ethnic group: (125) Contemporary Issues of Southeast Asian Refugees in the US and (132) Islamophobia and Constructing Otherness. The remaining courses are umbrella Asian American courses, but of course, all covering important issues within the community such as Asian Americans and Health or Asian Americans and Education. The content and extent to which these courses go into looking at specific ethnic communities is unknown. Under group 3 (cultural studies), we again see mostly umbrella Asian American courses in culture, literature, writing, etc. and the only specifics are of narratives on the Philippines and the US (unsure of allusion to Filipino-Americans or just the dynamics between the two), Chinese American, and Korean American—two of which are East Asian. Again, we cannot conclude that none of these courses do or do not delve deeper into diverse ethnic communities.

## Student Voice in AAADS

Beyond the current state of the department, the survey also asks for respondent voices on what changes or improvements they would like to see in the future of the AAADS department. Funding is a huge factor in making a lot of these changes happen, and many of the respondents have acknowledged this, but this is a whole other talk. However, if we exclude funding from the equation, many respondents asked for more community engagement:

*"I want the department to be vibrant and filled with professors of all topics who do community work and research, to have student voice present in the department, to have sustainable and consistent funding, to have more classes, and to have a strong community between other organizations, students, professors, and surrounding groups."*

*"[I want] more engagement with students and the community. I understand that professors are paid for research and the good name they give the academy through their research, but that's not a good reason to be disengaged from their students."*

At SF State, James Hirabayashi, serving as dean of the School of Ethnic Studies 1970-76, made an important point to mention the department's divergence from mainstream academics in that it considered communities of color proper objects of study and legitimate producers of knowledge. The Asian American studies curriculum was developed through close collaboration between students, faculty, and the community, and many courses were taught by community members without traditional academic credentials. (Daryl J. Maeda 69)

While professors push to have works of people of color and of our histories and experiences into the scholar world to prove that communities of color are "legitimate producers of knowledge", and students push to meet grades and requirements, we forget to communicate with each other and connect in a space that has been fought so hard for. "to have student voice present in the department" is reflective of one of the major reasons for the creation of Asian American Studies Students at Cal. The group aims to reintegrate student presence within the department rather than just as students in a classroom receiving material without the autonomy of deciding what they would like to learn and they would like to learn this. This continuous divide has slowly led to many students', specifically those majoring, minoring, or intending to be part of the AAADS department feel discouraged from joining the space.

Acknowledging that thoughts on changes would require suggestions of improvements, another question asked specifically about the classroom structure. About 2/3 of the survey respondents said that they would like to see more learning and discussion based courses that allows them to interact with the class where students can "learn from each other and discuss contemporary issues relating to the topic at hand" ("The Current & Future State of AAADS").

One respondent, again, mentions community work as being a significant part of the class and learning environment and requests that "the class be structured such that community work that we may already be engaged in is an integral part of the curriculum." Understandably, not everyone has the capacity to be involved with community work to a large extent, it is still a popular request to at least have the opportunities to begin to become involved.

Going back to the idea of active student participation in the department's discussion of which courses are to be offered, again with funding out of the equation, respondents were asked to recommend some potential topics that they would be interested in having offered through the department. These included topics such as Asian Americans and disability, Asian American literature in the 20$^{th}$ century (although there is a course that does offer this, but perhaps it is not as explicitly advertised as offering this capacity, which in that case would suggest that the department improve the way that classes are being presented), Asian American activism and art, Asian American food and its history/changes over time, Asian American folklore, and courses on specific Asian diasporic (e.g. Vietnamese, Cambodian, etc.) issues and how social/political context plays into their development in America. Though these are umbrella Asian American courses, which was disfavored earlier in the survey, these topics can be a start for where departments can consider looking into. An interesting respond was one respondent's wish for a course about "the future of Asian America: 3$^{rd}$ generation and beyond." We have focused so much on the history of Asian Americans and the generational gap between our Asian predecessors and Asian American offspring, but we have yet to cover "what next" as Asian America is not stagnant, and is instead continually moving towards the future with more generations.

Another response that stood out was that of one respondent who stated:

*"For me, as someone who wants to go into the healthcare field, there is a huge need for folx who are knowledgeable about issues that relate to the AAPI communities. AAADS classes would help me to understand these contemporary issues and the hxstory that allowed such issues to develop this way. Such knowledge is very helpful in caring for my future patients and other folx that I may care for and allow me to provide more culturally sensitive care."*

A huge majority of students today are part of the healthcare field, which makes sense that this respondent would bring up the importance of having AAADS classes that provides them with the background needed to approach AAPI community health issues. ASAMST 143AC, Asian Americans and Health, is a popular course that is offered through the AAADS department and increasingly with every semester, more and more students are put on the waitlist. There is talk that this course easily fulfills the AC requirement, but setting this aside, the structure of the course is ideal for many students in that they are able to learn about issues within the community as well as connect with guest speakers from the community if they were interested in continuing to be involved with the community.

As an important step forward, the AAADS department has recently approved of an unofficial certificate created and proposed by the Asian American

Pacific Islander Health Research Group (AAPIHRG) which signifies that the recipient of the certificate has taken courses that cover Asian American history, Asian American community health (ASAMST 143AC), taken the Break the Silence AAPIHRG decal about AAPI contemporary health issues, and has either done research or interned with the group. Having this certificate will hopefully bring in more interest to the department with the understanding that the health field, in fact, is an area of large interest.

Though the AAADS department, and Ethnic Studies, was created in order to create a space where people of color are producers of knowledge and to understand and analyze the diverse AAPI histories and experiences, some can say that there is a decline in the department which can be represented either in lack of funding, lack of student interest in courses, or lack of faculty. However, while many are fighting to continue to make presence within the scholarly world, it seems that understanding of current changes within the student and community spaces are looked over.

Courses that are being offered currently may be reflective of the original Asian American studies demands, but many of the courses, admittedly, may cover similar material and so, it would be more fruitful and impactful to have courses that are of specific interest to the current community. Course topics and syllabus or reading lists shouldn't need to be set in stone. For example, ASAMST 172 had a list of possible readings but depending on the demographic of the class, the readings were added or taken off the list in order for all students to be able to gain the most from their learning experience by integrating their own experiences. This course also created a space that was unlike many other courses in which every week was unplanned. Students come in after reading an assigned piece to discuss, but the discussion is completely student run.

This gives autonomy to the students to talk about what they got from the reading and how it relates to them rather than the goals or thoughts that the professor alone may have received from the reading. While some classes may not be as fluid as this in terms of their topics such as history dense courses, it is still more engaging to involve student voices in the discussion rather than just lecturing alone. This also gives the professors time to sit back and be part of the conversation rather than having to plan a set list of items to cover.

Opportunities to connect to the community was another big request from the respondents. While what is learned in the classroom is valuable and unique, it should be shared with the community who may not be able to access this same knowledge despite being the producers of the knowledge being studied. Moreover, in order for students to be able to engage with the community, there needs to be a bridge to the community from members who have already crossed that bridge. In that sense, a good model for that are courses in which guest speakers from the community are invited to the class or courses that offer field trips that require students to learn outside of the classroom.

There are a lot of gaps within the department-community relations as of lately, but this is where we should begin to look at what is causing these gaps and how to mend it. The survey used for this paper was mostly student opinionated, but for future work devoted to this cause, it would be of importance to also survey faculty and other members of the department as all sides of this conversation face their own difficulties and have individual perspectives.

## References

Dhingra, Pawan, and Robyn Magalit. Rodriguez. Asian America: Sociological and Interdisciplinary Perspectives. Polity Press, 2014.
Ha, Jacklin. "The Current & Future State of AAADS" Survey: https://tinyurl.com/ASAMST121Survey
Lee, Shelley Sang-Hee. A New History of Asian America. Routledge, Taylor & Francis Group, 2014.
Maeda, Daryl J. Chains of Babylon The Rise of Asian America. University of Minnesota Press, 2009.
Yu, Timothy. Has Asian American Studies Failed? Fordham University Press, 2018.

# School Communities/Community Schools

*LAILAN SANDRA HUEN*

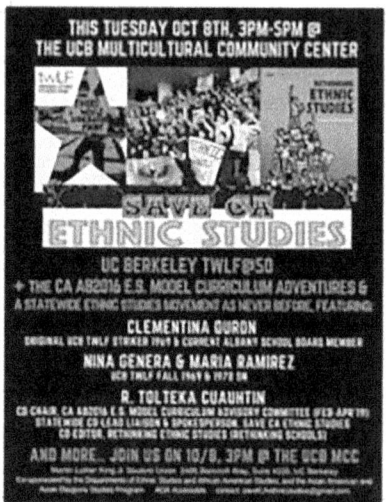

Photos left: Lailan Sandra Huen; Right: Poster, "Save CA Ethnic Studies" in secondary schools. 2019.

I was born from a love forged in the 1968 Third World Strike at UC Berkeley, as my parents helped create a new identity that my brother and I would later step into as Asian Americans. As they put their education and bodies on the line for our right to learn about our history, my parents and the other founders of Ethnic Studies sought to make relevant the resources of the university to communities in need right outside of its gates.

Growing up attending Oakland Unified School District (OUSD) public schools, aside from my one Asian American teacher who taught us about the Japanese internment and a third grade assignment on interviewing my grandparents, I never really had the opportunity to learn about my family and my community's history within the walls of the my schools. A Campfire Girls trip brought me to the Angel Island Immigration Station, and as I sat on its shores, for the first time in my memory, I began to more deeply understand the history of my family.

During my senior year at Skyline High School in the East Oakland hills, race riots between Asian American and Black students broke out. My peers and I quickly realized that our 12-year education had not educated us on the stories of our diverse student body which was in one of the most diverse and integrated cities in the world. More importantly, while we were struggling over trigonometry and grammar, we were never taught the tools or language to navigate the complex race relations which would explode in that year. Even though Ethnic Studies was founded in universities 20 years prior, the vast knowledge documented and uncovered by new scholarship had never made it to our K-12 public school textbooks and curriculum.

It turned out that New York City became my best lab for learning and understanding the world. Protests of the Amadou Diallo verdict erupted during my freshman year at Columbia. I became involved with CAAAV: Organizing Asian Communities and collaborated with the burgeoning Domestic Workers United movement for my senior thesis and Masters project. However, Columbia taught me a language that was not accessible to the communities in New York City, and my thesis and papers never helped anyone but myself. I was never encouraged towards the incredible opportunity to be of better use to communities that needed documentation, knowledge production and voice.

Wary of the university's politics, I shunned academia and dove into the on-the-ground organizing for various efforts including the fight against the prison industrial complex and educational justice for public schools being closed. My learning community became the movements around me, as I learned to apply knowledge and utilize resources from educational institutions for the purpose of serving nearby communities. In 2007, our East Oakland Community High School, the one place I have seen the effective engagement of former gang members and diverse teachers, was closed by state administrators who believed that playing hip hop in school meant that students were not learning. My work in education found young leaders in leadership and afterschool programs where students created the space to develop their voice and agency. The self-efficacy skills developed in those programs lacked in their traditional classrooms.

In 2010, Superintendent Tony Smith declared that Oakland schools will be Community Schools working to address student needs with wrap-around services. Educators like myself found that finally, everything we had been fighting for over the past several decades found itself into the OUSD's official strategic plan and vision. Smith called for African American Male Achievement programs, which then spurred the creation of an Office of Equity in 2017, where I now work in curating Asian Pacific Islander Student Achievement Programs for our most struggling API students. Like Ethnic Studies programs, this effort continues to be called into question and put onto the budget chopping block, especially by white staff who fail to understand the need for targeted universalism and race-conscious programs. In addition, we have received very little district funds for targeting programming.

50 years later, Ethnic Studies classes are now available for 9th grade students at most OUSD high schools, yet they are not mandatory. A small handful of OUSD staff have forged these Ethnic Studies programs with little funding and few grants. These educators built the requirement for every senior to conduct Senior Projects examining an issue in their community, which is one of the most powerful Ethnic Studies projects now implemented.

Textbooks are still pretty exclusive of much history of communities of color in the United States and the world. Teachers are still disproportionately white and struggle with connecting and understanding their students. In many classes, worksheets and stale assignments still dominate learning formats. Social justice pathways struggle to maintain funding and support. Accounting for over 125 ethnic groups in Oakland, most students yearn for Ethnic Studies and culturally responsive curriculum.

In 2017, a film about the Chinese Exclusion Act was released. OUSD partnered with the Center for Asian American Media to develop school curriculum that finally made visible the long and unspoken history of Chinese Americans in the United States since the Gold Rush. It was only after the film when I learned the context and stories of my great-grandfathers who came to San Francisco Chinatown, Oakland Chinatown and Mexicali under the threat of racist immigration policies and anti-Asian violence which had culminated in the 1882 Exclusion Act. It was only then that I truly understood my role in the world, at age 35.

In overall K-12 education, there remains much work to be done to break down the barriers between our education institutions and our communities. In 2019, the State of California Department of Education will finally develop a model curriculum for Ethnic Studies, providing hope that somewhere in the near future, our students will be able to learn about themselves, their families and communities, and their role in the world as well.

# Jumping into the River of Justice

*KAI NHAM*

*April 24, 2019.*

*Left: Kai Nham. Right: Kai Nham, second from right at Mountain Movers book event. October 28, 2019.*

In 1969, my ba was born into a war torn Việt Nam in Sóc Trăng. That same year, the Third World Liberation Front (TWLF) struggled and fought for Third World studies at the University of California, Berkeley. In 1970, my ma was born in pre-handover Hong Kong. That same year, the first Asian American and Ethnic Studies courses were taught at Berkeley. All would reach out across time and deeply shape the young person I am and will continue to grow to be. Marking the fiftieth anniversary of TWLF, I walked across the stage and graduated with a degree in Asian American Studies from a department that has drastically changed.

And as I walked, I thought about the elders who fought for the seat I occupied and never graduated with their own degree. I thought about the tear gas, the police terror, and the backlash. I thought about my family fleeing Việt Nam and China – how three generations would never know the same home. I thought about how I never learned any of these histories growing up and how the depths of these silences were a complex violence I still have no language for. But I also thought about the joy, the laughter, the friendships that ran deep in TWLF. I thought about the resilience of my family and my communities, how I learned tenderness and abundance in so many different ways. These are the contradictions I held as I crossed that stage, the contradictions I still sit with as I sit down to write this.

The legacy of TWLF has imparted in me a deep love and commitment to liberation and community that transcend mere bureaucratic demands. Maybe reflective of what the Ethnic Studies department has become, I learned very few things in the classrooms I studied in. But it gave me an entry point into the spaces of learning and growth that our elders imagined: my community. I have learned so much from my elders, my comrades, and the youth, and I have been forever changed. Yet, as I move forward in my journey, I continue to wonder how Third World studies can be manifested the way that TWLF imagined it.

Pam Tau Lee once said to the youth at Chinese Progressive Association – San Francisco, "Are you willing to jump into the river of justice even if you may never see the ocean?" And that's the commitment I have made, regardless of the degree. Third World studies asks me – asks us – to continue this labor of love, to continue to believe in building a movement that can hold all of the abundance and fullness of our beings. I walked away with a degree but came away with things that no institution could teach me: the power of love and community.

*LaNada War Jack visits Eastwind Books of Berkeley holding copy of Stand Up. January 2019. Harvey Dong photo.*

# We Need to Learn From What Happened

JOANNE YI

*May 30, 2019*

*Joanne Yi speaking on Sproul Steps during TWLF 50th. January 22, 2019. Harvey Dong photo.*

My name is Joanne Yi. I use She and They pronouns. I just graduated, finally, after three years. I've been an AAADS (Asian American and Asian Diaspora Studies) major since the end of my first year when I decided to major in AAADS. My choice of major had to do with my upbringing in Stockton, California, where there once had been the largest population of Filipinos outside the Philippines. I didn't grow up knowing that until I became aware in high school through the destruction of Little Manila and the Crosstown Freeway, which divided Stockton into North and South. North Stockton is predominantly White and wealthy, and South Stockton is people of color. My family was one of the few Korean-Americans there. So I grew up around Filipinos, Hmong and Sikh children. I felt very connected to a Pan Asian American identity. Also, people mistook my family as being Chinese or Japanese because of their historical presence in Stockton. I understood that to White society, it didn't really matter whether or not I was Korean. It just mattered how they saw me as Asian.

Growing up in the wealthier white neighborhood of North Stockton but having a very diverse group of close friends who were from all over Stockton and South Stockton, I realized that there was a lot of disparity in access to resources. From my own family's experience, I saw that there was deep racism and oppression within Stockton. I came to college with the idea that I wanted to learn more about oppression and how to fight that oppression. I wanted to come to college to learn about my community and bring those skills and those resources back to my community. I think because when I was in high school I saw Dr. Dawn Mabalon and others who were five to six years older than me coming back to Stockton, I felt that's what I wanted to do with my education.

When I came to Berkeley, I wanted to learn more about social justice. I was a Philosophy major at first and thought about Political Science as well. My social justice education was actually from on-campus organizing. I was introduced to REACH, the Asian Pacific Islander Recruitment Retention Center; and in the annual Central California Outreach trip in which a group of Berkeley students and other college students go to high schools in the Central Valley to talk about higher education.

I met other students involved in on campus Asian-American organizing in REACH and groups like SASC, the Southeast Asian Student Coalition. I had also met a few Asian American and Asian Diaspora Studies majors when I was a freshman who encouraged me to go on the Central California Outreach trip. Stockton itself is in the Central Valley and recruitment there had been deeply neglected.

I thought about the oppression I witnessed there and I wanted to find a way to go back. The fact that there was a group of college students on campus here at Berkeley who were organizing a trip, inspired me and I immediately connected to REACH. I went on that trip and I eventually became an intern in the Spring semester of my Freshman year. That became my introduction to the bigger on campus organizing space. As a REACH intern, I was in the Political Advocacy Team. Our responsibility was to do more community organizing work. Our team established the MOVE fellowship. Based on the principles of the Third World Liberation Front and Asian American Studies, we wanted to find a way for student organizers to gain experience and contribute what they learned to community organizations around the Bay Area. We wanted to acquire training in community organizing, because student organizing and off campus organizing are very different. So, we found a way to bridge the two. We started that fellowship with community organizations in the Bay: the Chinese Progressive Association, Asian Pacific Environmental Network (APEN) and Asian Youth Political Action League (AYPAL).

What we learned on campus shouldn't be isolated to campus and what we learned in the classroom should be applied practically. I didn't actually take my first Asian American Studies class or Ethnic Studies class until the following semester in my Sophomore year. I thought the classes would be imbued with the organizing ideas that we had been practicing, Serve the People and de-colonial education. But I found something very different.

I thought that the founding principles of Ethnic Studies and the Third World Liberation Front, which I learned about in REACH and from professors like Professor Harvey Dong, would offer engaging classes, a space for students to share narratives, to critique and challenge power, and especially how we could continue that off campus. But I found the classes, the department, the program instead looked inward and focused on academics which in many ways reproduced the power structures that we were supposed to be dismantling.

But I decided to continue on as a major anyway, though the program wasn't what I wanted or what I needed out of my education. I felt I was developing politically and critically off campus within the community organizations which I worked. When I worked with AYPAL off campus, first as an intern and then later as a staffer, I -learned a lot about the history of the Asian American Movement, particularly because these organizations had come out of that movement. And I was also learning that the theories we learned in class, like the Model Minority Myth, were playing out in real time, affecting communities. I felt the urgency of my education was there. What I learned from off-campus spaces and from organizing, I wrote about in my campus class papers. I didn't formally learn a lot in classes. My primary education was from the community.

While the bulk of my social justice education took place off-campus in community organizing, there still remained an important need for our classes to keep up with contemporary issues. I think that what is unique about Asian American Studies and also about Ethnic Studies on college campuses is that there's a large population of people who want to learn about these issues for the first time. If we don't offer quality classes that critique power, then we are doing them a disservice. Students get the idea that learning about their own history isn't important and challenging current oppression isn't a priority.

## Setting Out to Change the Program and Department

When I was a Sophomore in 2017, we set out to change both the program and the department. I got together with a group of other Ethnic Studies students who had been organizing and we had strategy meetings to decide how to move forward. We eventually decided that we were going to present a letter to the chair of the Ethnic Studies department, basically telling them about our grievances and hoping to open up a conversation about how we wanted to move forward. If you see the letter or read the letter, it's very much a letter that comes out of love and emphasizes the original principles of the Third Liberation Front. We were saying: "why aren't our classes reflecting the urgency that we feel in our communities?" and "why aren't we getting the social justice education that we deserve?" We were concerned about the quality of classes, the quantity of classes, and the structure. We wanted to continue moving forward on the idea of a Third World College and to push forward the conversation.

We wrote the letter and we got Ethnic Studies students together to present the letter with us. Obviously if it had been one or two students who went to the chair of the department, it would have been shut down. In fact, we had sent it to her multiple times and tried to set up a formal meeting. She just kept dodging us and ignoring us. We felt that we had no other option but to go in person and to present the letter. And we needed community pressure to make sure that the department chair actually listened to us. I couldn't be there when we presented the letter, but I had been a part of the planning process.

There was a Facebook video that went around of the letter presentations to the chair and a few professors. Apparently, some professors later felt like they had been threatened or that their safety was in danger. But I think if you look at the video there are multiple times in which people are checking with the professor, asking her if she's okay, and she said that she was. And so, the narrative that was constructed after the fact was to demonize students and say that we were being aggressive, an interesting way to characterize a bunch of students of color who had legitimate grievances and had been trying to repeatedly get in touch with the chair. So, this was obviously an escalation of the situation by those professors.

After that action in which we presented the letter, there was a lot of backlash, particularly against the student organizers. The student action happened in November of 2017, and around January or February in 2018, many of the student organizers received an email from the Dean of Student Affairs saying that one of their staff members wanted to meet with us. We were really concerned. Particularly when I got the email, I wanted to know how they knew that I had been part of the planning process, because I wasn't there.

There were rumors that other professors were being asked to identify key student organizers from the Facebook video, and to basically say that these students were leading the student revolution, and that they should be punished. And then there were also rumors that professors were trying to get us expelled or to have us punished or to even have us arrested. And so, I think all this, in the time from November to June, sowed a lot of discomfort and paranoia, particularly among student organizers. There was also a rumor that there was a student mole in our group, that somebody had been planted there by professors to report back on what the students were doing. We felt a high sense of paranoia and our organizing group disbanded.

We tried to take care of each other and those concerned they were going to be expelled. Students in Ethnic Studies are predominantly low-income students of color and the first in their family generations to be in college. Going to college is seen as a way out of poverty for themselves and their families. These students felt that to jeopardize their position here at the university would be to jeopardize their entire family's stability, and they wanted to stay in the university. These were the fears we faced when we got those emails from the Dean of Student Affairs. We wanted to try and keep as low of a profile as possible. So, we went through the process. I met with one of the staff members from the Dean of Student Affairs who basically just wanted to let me know what my rights were, but this was obviously an intimidation tactic to say: "you are going to get in trouble if you do this again!" I think that that was probably a compromise between professors who probably wanted something more extreme to happen and professors who wanted to protect us. The Dean of Student Affairs meeting was probably the compromise that they came up with. But either way, it still really intimidated and scared a lot of students. And so, we didn't continue any further than the letter delivery.

From the time that I came to Berkeley, up until the moment that I graduated, I've never known a time in which Ethnic Studies students felt positively about the department. When we did the letter delivery, we actually didn't have to put in an extensive amount of work to organize or mobilize students to come with us. It's like in a drop of a hat, Ethnic Studies students are ready to advocate for a Third World College and further their education. The letter didn't even have a list of demands. It was basically an invitation to open up conversation about how students and professors could be working together, particularly against the university administration, to advocate on behalf of all of us. Up until that point, we had conceptualized the main barrier to a Third World college and the wellness of the Ethnic Studies programs, was the university admission, and the head of the College of Letters and Sciences.

But I think because of the internal backlash we received from professors, we realized that we were also fighting amongst ourselves, students versus professors, in some cases, professors against professors. We revealed a lot more of the internal dynamics going on and the internal conflicts. For me and for a lot of other students, the fact that professors didn't support us was very surprising and in a lot of ways more hurtful, because these were the people that we were interacting with the most.

I think that we also felt more paranoid because we had to continue taking classes with these professors. And so that's part of the reason why we decided to tread a little bit more lightly. But one thing that came out of that conflict was that students had a very clear understanding of where each professor stood; whether they supported us or whether they didn't support us. And also, it became clear to us the internal power dynamics of the department amongst professors, which tenured faculty glued together to hold the power within the department and who was on the outskirts, how lecturers are treated. From then on, for me, the only people that I could really trust were gonna be lecturers who were put on the outskirts of the department, and that tenured faculty were not to be trusted at all. Moving forward, I felt a lot of hurt and paranoia, especially about the mole. I thought about dropping out of school altogether. But I didn't want to feel like I had lost to the Ethnic Studies professors, so I decided to stay in school. My next closest option was to transfer out of the major, but I ultimately decided to just continue in the major and graduate a year earlier than planned in Spring 2019.

# Ethnic Studies Graduation Speech: 50 Means Hope

RIZZA ESTACIO

*Undergraduate Graduation Speaker, Spring 2019.*

Good Afternoon graduates, family, friends, faculty, and staff. Welcome to the Ethnic Studies Commencement! Every commencement is special, but this one in particular is very special. This year marks the 50th anniversary of the Third World Liberation strikes, the student protests that gave way to the founding of the Ethnic Studies department. I learned the history of what it meant to be the 50th in classes and in books, but I learned what it really meant to be 50th, what it represented and the weight that it held, in a very different sort of place.

    I shelve books, count money and take out the trash at Eastwind Books on University Avenue. It is a place filled to the brim with books; of history and narrative and how to cook and how to speak and how to read. We have countless books on topics from decolonizing your diet to teaching your five-year-old what anarchy is. My bosses are two of the sweetest and ripest people on the block, who I call my Berkeley grandparents. There is Bea who studied Ethnic Studies and English in 1969, and Harvey who studied Ethnic Studies at UC Berkeley around the same time. 1969. They tell me stories of 1969. They tell me stories of the strike that shook the world of academia and of the veterans of the strike that they know.

On some odd Sundays a bunch of elders pile into the store, sharing pork and taro buns in the back, while I ring up the customers. I hear their laughter, their joy of being able to see each other and acknowledge that they haven't changed so much after all. I hear their remorse, the recognition of all the sacrifices piled into being students fighting their university, for what, the academic recognition they and their people always deserved.

I hear their desire, to keep on fighting and keep on educating new generations of radical, hard-headed, kind-hearted student leaders to keep on demanding for everything that got left out. Harvey and Bea tell me somber stories about the man who got arrested and beaten by the police for non-violently striking, and softly smile when they reflect on his life now, owning a successful small business, selling tortillas to taco trucks in Hawaii.

They tell me about the woman who organized sit ins and believed in the power in disobedience, who is now a school principal because she continues to believe that discipline and punishment should never be responses to a young person refusing to abide to unfairness. They tell me about the leaders of the strike, who in the midst of organizing, and protesting, and sit ins, and poster making, fell in love — and live and love all of their notions of what it means to be radical through raising a family and settling down. They tell me about the young people they knew, who became the elders that they know, and how you never grow out of radicalism even if it presents itself in the most untraditional of ways.

You can make tortillas, or become a school principal, or own a small bookstore and be a foundational part of the resistance against all that is wrong with our world. You can do all of these things and be a radical, and never let the radical parts of you die.

I think to my own classmates, who are now my young people friends, but in what will most likely feel like a blink of an eye, will come elders like Harvey and Bea's friends, who will be brimming with wisdom and awe at the world.

I think of Tasha, a graduate student in Native American Studies, whose Ph.D is in language revitalization on the Standing Rock Indian Reservation in North and South Dakota. Before I met Tasha, who was my graduate student instructor for 101B, she was at Standing Rock, working in schools making sure that while community members were organizing against the construction of the Dakota access pipeline, things like schools and children services could still be open and running. She taught my class about motif and narrative structure, that organizing looks like a protest and being on the ground. But it also looks like the ever important "background work", taking care of the children, and educating them to be the next generation of radicals. Tasha's dissertation work is just as astounding as her community work that collects the knowledge necessary to preserve indigenous languages; meanwhile establishing that while so many people mistake Native American studies to be a discipline of far off history, in actuality, it is a field of ever growing, contemporary knowledges and a culmination of ancestral and community work and academic discovery.

I think of my friend, the brilliant, Karen Ni, who studies Asian American Diaspora Studies, and wants to change the way we see the world through multimedia. After learning about the decades of propaganda that has been used by white supremacy to degrade Asian American communities, they want to work for ad agencies and morph our mind around what multicultural America really looks like. They want to make billboards with people of color on them. They want to force large companies to reflect on the demographics they are failing to reach, and they want to use mass consumed art to open people's eyes to the injustices around them.

I think of my friend studying Chicanx/Latinx studies, whose passions were awoken by reading the narratives of intersectional feminists and whose minds and body and heart were touched by reading for the first time in their entire life about the intersections of woman hood, queerness and brownness. For the first time, they felt whole by something academic. They are passionate about becoming a lawyer and advocating for women and sex workers and femmes and non-binary peoples and bringing justice to people that get left in the margins too often.

I think of one of my best friends Juniper Angelica Cordova, but you might just know her as Gia, who studies comparative Ethnic Studies. She is going to be the first woke president of the United States. She is going to destroy prisons and ICE, and channel the military funds into health care funds. She is going to end world hunger and labor malpractices, and she's going to save us all. While looking absolutely fabulous.

I think about all of us, who are every second traversing on the long road to becoming some other generations' elders, and what kind of wisdom we will impart. I think about what it means to change the world whether you make tortillas, or shelve books, or become a civil rights lawyer, or a kindergarten teacher. I think about the endlessness of this road, where our world ends, and where the next generation begins.

I think about 50. What 50 means to me, to us.

I think about 50 more years of this department. I'm an idealist, and this is a moment of celebration so appease me on this. In 50 years, I don't see a department, I see a Third World College, large enough to swallow the stage of Zellerbach Hall, whose seating capacity triples this. In 50 years, I see a department that doesn't struggle for funding and can double its faculty so we can expand in the types of knowledge that we proliferate. In 50 years, I see a department that has the stability and funding to re-join with African American studies, so instead of just learning about the struggles of Black people, we can study with and learn from them as faculty. In 50 years, I see a department that has learned from past shortcomings, that has syllabi filled with the work of Central American and Pacific Islander scholars who get left off of our reading lists too often, and centers the history, policy, and scholarship of those who live at the intersections of being people of color and all of their other identities. In 50 more, I see us growing, sprouting new flowers, our roots reaching into the foundation of the university.

I think about what 50 means for us. In 50 more years, I see our revolution coming into fruition. I know it takes work, but how can I stand here and pretend that something big and amazing isn't going to happen with all of the brilliant minds that sit on this stage being released into the worlds of academia, education, law, policy, and the medical field. I know the revolution takes work; I can assure you that the Ethnic Studies class of 2019 is up to the challenge.

I think about what 50 means for me. I hope that I am still writing, and I have half the knowledge my mentor and thesis advisor has. Thank you, Beth. You are such a brilliant and powerful individual; you have made my Berkeley experience beautiful. I don't think I would be such a passionate or intellectual student if it wasn't for you. In 50 years, I hope I have half the wisdom of my parents, who are in the audience today. Thanks mom and dad, and lola. Neither of you had the privilege to do what I'm doing today, and I am so thankful for every sacrifice you've made. I know I have a piece of paper signed by random white people that tells me that I'm a smart person, but I hope I can one day have half of the brilliance that you both have.

All in all, I think 50 means hope. I think that the class of 69 hoped for something like this to happen, and this was in a lot of ways their wildest dream. Their labor, their strife, their tears, the sit ins, the protests, the arrests, the sacrifices: the seeds. We: the flowers. I am in joy and satisfaction and in tears watching us bloom. Congratulations class of 2019 and 69 and everyone in between, we did it!

*Representing generations: TWLF/twLF 1969/1999/2009/2017. Multicultural Community Center. October 6, 2018. Doug Parada photo.*

# Chapter Four:
# Celebrating 50 Years of Ethnic Studies

# Embracing the Politics of Education: Celebrating 50 Years of Ethnic Studies as a Praxis of Liberation

ZIZA DELGADO

Left: Ziza Delgado. Right: TWLF strikers and supporters, 1969. Doug Wachter photo.

*"During decolonization the people were called upon to fight against the oppression. Following national liberation, they are urged to fight against poverty, illiteracy, and under development. The struggle, they say, goes on. The people realize that life is an unending struggle."*

*Frantz Fanon, The Wretched of the Earth (2004, page 51)*

2018 marked the 50th anniversary of one of the most tumultuous years in American history, a year that shaped the politics of both the left and right for decades to come. From the Tet Offensive, which shattered the American government's narrative that the United States (U.S.) was winning the war in Vietnam, to the assassination of Martin Luther King Jr., 1968 exposed the violent failures of American imperialism abroad as well as the homegrown terrorism that is white supremacy. 2018-2019 also represents the 50th anniversary of the Third World Liberation Front (TWLF) movement that ushered in the creation of Ethnic Studies. To tell the history of how Ethnic Studies came into existence requires centralizing the role of students and young people who successfully demanded a radical concession of space and power from institutions that only mildly tolerated their presence. From its inception, the field of Ethnic Studies has existed and has been sustained, because of the students committed to its vision and mission. This chapter is dedicated to the elders who founded our field and all the students who have risked their education, and often their bodies, to sustain it.

On November 6, 1968, students, faculty, staff, and community members of color at San Francisco State University (SFSU) initiated the first TWLF movement for Ethnic Studies. This five-month student strike, which effectively prevented the college from functioning, was the longest student strike in U.S. history. The efforts of the SFSU TWLF movement successfully led to the creation of the first and only College of Ethnic Studies. The legacy of the SFSU strike, initiated by the Black Student Union with the support of the Black Panther Party, cannot be understated. The Black Student Union/TWLF activism provided a framework and model for students of color dedicated to fighting for Ethnic Studies by any means necessary. The impact of this achievement reverberated throughout higher education, beginning with neighboring Bay Area universities and spreading across the country. Gaining institutional representation and validation, the TWLF movements secured a radical victory for members of marginalized communities in their effort to achieve power in one area of their lives - education. The leadership and revolutionary activism of the TWLF student movements are more than an inspiring or even a transformative event in education, they represent a culminating moment of victory for historically marginalized communities in the U.S.

## The TWLF at UC Berkeley and the Longue Durée of Ethnic Studies

Across the Bay, at UC Berkeley, Black students in the Afro-American Student Union were energized by the developments at SFSU. Since November 1968, they had been in conversation with the University about their own demands for a Black Studies department. By January 1969, after months of failed negotiations, Black students mobilized with Asian, Latinx, and Native American students who were ready to unite after months of activism in their own communities. Under the umbrella organization known as the Third World Liberation Front, in solidarity with SFSU, the struggle for Ethnic Studies emerged on January 21, 1969 at UC Berkeley.

The formation of the TWLF was not only a product of the radical milieu of the 1960s, but also part of a much longer history of resistance that includes rebellions both large and small against slavery and Indigenous resistance to colonization. A particularly relevant precursor to the TWLF movement that also saw education as a path to freedom and a form of liberation for those long denied access to literacy and formal education took place during the Reconstruction

Era and was led by the Black community to create the first universal system of public education for themselves in the South (Anderson, 1995). James D. Anderson (1995) argues that in the post-emancipation South, Black educators "emerged from among the rebel literates...slaves who had sustained their own learning process in defiance of the slave owner's authority" (p. 17). The rebellious nature of these leaders further signifies a strong tradition of Black educators resisting white supremacy. Using a longue durée[55] framework highlights how the racism, exploitation and violence that communities of color were challenging in the 1960s, both on and off college campuses, were inherited traits of a society diseased from chattel slavery, genocide, orientalism, and capitalism. The 1960s represents a powerful moment in world history because oppressed people found solidarity in their experiences and converged to form a constellation of struggle (Johnson G.T., 2008) around many issues. From the support that Third World nations provided each other as they broke free of their colonizers to the interracial coalitions that formed around the Civil Rights and labor movements, the comradery that emerged during this era radically shifted the global politics and power structure, even if temporarily and incompletely[56]. In the case of the TWLF, this solidarity focused on claiming space and institutional power in the form of Ethnic Studies.

The TWLF at UC Berkeley had one broad goal that served as the umbrella under which all other demands fell: self-determination. Most people assume that the demands of the TWLF prioritized creating politically and culturally relevant courses, considering this has been the area in which their movement has perhaps had the most visible impact. However, their primary concern originated from their call for self-determination, which at UC Berkeley was defined as proportional representation of people of color in the university; recognition of Third World peoples' histories; Third World control of their new space (college or department); and making the university accountable to serve the needs of Third World communities.[57] Their framing of self-determination went

---

55  Published in 1949, this concept was developed by the French historian Fernand Braudel. The emphasis of this approach is dialectical: it is about how the history of the past informs the present. This is an interdisciplinary method of examining and revealing how long-term political, social, and economic structures impact our social reality today (Lee, 2012).
56  Many of these radical movements were weakened by both external forces, such as the FBI's COINTELPRO program, or internal divisions, such as the sexism and homophobia that was prevalent in many of these struggles. Additionally, the collective Third World dreams that emerged from the Bandung (1955) and Havana (1966) conferences have been largely dismantled, due to both crushing debt and the failure of many of the once-revolutionary leaders to translate those freedoms won during decolonization into real change for the majority of their poor populations (Prashad, 2007).
57  Third World Strike at University of California, Berkeley collection, CES ARC 2015/1 Ethnic Studies Library, University of California, Berkeley. Location: 1.71 TWLF box 1 Folder 71 1969 - Publications pamphlets. p. 4.

even further to include a longue durée analysis of racism in the U.S. In their pamphlet entitled "The Strike Explained" they identified self-determination as their overarching goal, under which all other demands fell. They stated:

> *The TWLF is demanding the end of all forms of racism in the university. The end of racism requires first of all that Third World peoples are proportionately represented in terms of faculty, administrators, and specific numbers of admissions. But the TWLF is demanding far more than that; they are demanding 'self-determination.' This means a recognition that racism in America has involved not only economic deprivation and the failure of white society to provide Third World people with a meaningful education, but also the systemic destruction of whole peoples and the deliberate attempt for more than three hundred years to obliterate the basic sense of dignity of entire groups of people...*[58]

In this 16-page document the TWLF articulates the grievances of both students and the communities they come from to explain the role that higher education has played in causing harm and why Ethnic Studies is part of addressing that history. Never before have the elite, predominately White, institutions of the American higher education system been forced to consider the demands and intellectual contributions of this population. These demands regarding race, space, and institutional power reflect one of the most important and lasting contributions TWLF has had in academia.

The demands of the TWLF, and even the more concrete call for a college of Ethnic Studies, were often dismissed as utopian fantasies. Thus, in their efforts to lay out their vision for the proposed College of Ethnic Studies, again inspired by the SFSU movement, the TWLF activists at UC Berkeley allowed themselves to dream of a future they wanted that did not yet exist. It is important to acknowledge that the pedagogy that was practiced during the establishment of Ethnic Studies was aligned with the teaching of Paulo Freire, famed Brazilian educator and philosopher, despite TWLF organizers not having been exposed to his work yet (it had not yet been translated from Portuguese). Freire's (1996) own words are helpful here for understanding the sentiment and vision behind the TWLF's call for an education for oppressed people: "I can't respect the teacher who doesn't dream of a certain kind of society that he would like to live in, and like a new generation to live in; a dream of society

---

[58] Third World Strike at University of California, Berkeley collection, CES ARC 2015/1 Ethnic Studies Library, University of California, Berkeley. Location: 1.71 TWLF box 1 Folder 71 1969 - Publications pamphlets. p. 4.

less ugly than we have today" (Freire, 1996, as cited in O'Donnell et al., 2004, p. 34). Thus, in their efforts to establish Ethnic Studies as an innovative and radical field and create a physical space to house it at UC Berkeley, the TWLF movement engaged the institution in their vision of decolonization. This goal would prove to be difficult in practice as it often put the emerging discipline in opposition to the power structure it had become a part of. However, that spirit of decolonization did successfully influence the course content and ideology of the department as it was establishing itself.

The impact that decolonization movements in the Third World had on Ethnic Studies is evidenced by the deeply anti-colonial discourse adopted by the TWLF, by their support and alignment with revolutionaries fighting worldwide for independence, and ultimately in their curriculum. For example, two courses offered from 1970-1980 were "African Liberation Movements," that studied "the philosophies, strategies, and tactics of the African Liberation Movements in Southern Africa,"[59] and "Colonialism and Internal Colonialism," that offered students the opportunity to survey the "major writings dealing with the experience of Third World people under colonialism."[60] These courses, and the majority of the curriculum in the first decade, was unapologetically political. As faculty and students who were living through the largest decolonization era in modern world history, they prioritized teaching and learning about those movements in real time and forging solidarity with other oppressed people. For example, in the first UC Berkeley Ethnic Studies Department course catalogue for spring 1970 what is striking is the art they selected, which portrays revolutionary images of Vietcong fighters, the Mayan calendar, a clenched fist, phrases reading "Free Alcatraz," and beautiful images of African and Indigenous symbolism. These images are important to analyze because they represent the affinity the department had for Third World culture and radical politics and how they materialized that into a document put on display for all the University to see and one designed to recruit potential majors.

Additionally, the Ethnic Studies Department's choice to continue to use the term "Third World" to describe communities of color in the U.S. in their curricula up until the 1980s, despite the shifting discourse in the U.S. at the time, reflects their ongoing commitment to the radical politics of decolonization, from which the department was conceived. Use of the term "Third World" in reference to oppressed communities of color in the U.S. was an intentional

---

[59] "Afro-American Studies 1-155" Request for Approval or Withdrawal of a Course Forms University Archives Records Collection. Berkeley: The Bancroft Library, University of California, Berkeley. n.d. CU-9, Box 8282.2. Print.

[60] Course Catalogue "Department of Ethnic Studies, 1979-1980." Ethnic Studies Library-not catalogued.

political position that aligned with theories of internal colonialism (Blauner, 1969), and ultimately with the logic of anti-colonial rebellion, further differentiating Ethnic Studies' politics from other disciplines. As a field, Ethnic Studies saw its role in student's lives as more than just intellectual work but rather as practical training to prepare students to change the material conditions in their communities. The concept of liberation became a reality in the 1950s and 1960s for many former colonies and this permeated the imagination of people of color world-wide. The TWLF's commitment to creating their own educational space reflected this monumental ideological shift. Here, Freire's notion of the utopian ideal was reflected in the creation of Ethnic Studies because the TWLF knew that dismantling the systems, structures, and ideologies that supported the long history of oppression and exploitation of people of color required imagining an education drastically different than what they were offered in the traditional academic disciplines.

Ethnic Studies was not created as simply an addition to the Eurocentric tradition within the academy. It was designed with a clear and unrelenting commitment to correct the ahistorical, inaccurate, and racist "research" that permeated every aspect of public life, especially academia. The TWLF was explicitly committed to creating an educational space different from anything at UC Berkeley or in the American education system in general. In the United States, the dominant education system has been shown to reproduce social inequality (Althusser, 1974; Bowles & Gintis, 1976; Fischer et al., 1996; Woodson, 1933; Blau & Duncan, 1967). Alternatively, the TWLF movements for Ethnic Studies established priorities to radically disrupt this process and make education a tool for the empowerment of historically marginalized peoples through a curriculum and praxis that valued their communities' contributions, struggles, and by having students work in service of and in solidarity with local organizations and movements in the Bay Area. Despite the budget cuts, tenuous relationships with those in power, the institutional appropriation, and at times de-radicalization that Ethnic Studies has experienced at UC Berkeley and many other campuses, it remains the first academic discipline created as a result of student activism and thus its perseverance for the last 50 years deserves celebration and study.

## The Politics of an Ethnic Studies Education in the 21st Century

In my contribution to this anthology, I want to honor the labor and sacrifices made by our elders and subsequent generations of activists in the TWLF movements who fought against so many odds to create a space for historically marginalized people in the academy. As a professor of Ethnic Studies and an educator who values and uses critical pedagogical strategies in my teaching, I am guided by a commitment to practicing 'education as liberation,' a call that was at the heart of the TWLF movement. In her widely read reflection on the spirit and motivations of a pedagogy of liberation, esteemed scholar and cultural critic bell hooks (1994) stated:

> *To educate as the practice of freedom is a way of teaching that anyone can learn. That learning process comes easiest to those of us who teach who also believe that there is an aspect of our vocation that is sacred; who believe that our work is not merely to share information but to share in the intellectual and spiritual growth of our students. To teach in a manner that respects and cares for the souls of our students is essential if we are to provide the necessary conditions where learning can most deeply and intimately begin (hooks, 1994, p. 13).*

This call to educators reflects not only what was at the heart of the Black education movement during Reconstruction but also the essence of what makes Ethnic Studies so unique in the American education system. Born out of a movement driven by a pedagogy of liberation, the field and discipline of Ethnic Studies has contributed to the development of a unique and protective relationship between Ethnic Studies students and the Ethnic Studies learning spaces that they hold sacred. Indeed, the care and nurturing based on the communion between educator and student in Ethnic Studies learning spaces, and that which is described by hooks (1994) above has generated and supported justice-oriented transformation and activism for decades.

*Posters from TWLF 40<sup>th</sup> in 2009. Courtesy of Manuel Delgado.*

Through all the transitions that Ethnic Studies at UC Berkeley experienced in the last 50 years, one constant has been the role that students have played in sustaining the department. One of the most unique components of an Ethnic Studies education is the relationship its students have to sustaining the field. Ethnic Studies at UC Berkeley has its current staff, resources, and community space because of the protest that its students have carried out to defend and strengthen it. In 1999, student organizing and an effective a hunger strike successfully resuscitated the department after years of it being deprived of full time hires and funding, the pillars that uphold any discipline in the academy. Other achievements of the 1999 UC Berkeley strike include the creation of the Multicultural Community Center and Center for Race and Gender. These two centers still provide resources and serve as critical spaces of representation and knowledge production on campus. In 2011, our students again went on a hunger strike to protest the austerity measures imposed by the university which sought to cut our departmental staff and ignore the services we provide to students of color across campus. With each of these contemporary protests, students have invoked the legacy of the TWLF in their activism. They have done this by introducing the movement and teaching its origins to a new generation of students and forcing the university to address the grievances of marginalized students, faculty, and staff.

In May of 2016, four students at San Francisco State University, Hassani Bell, Ahkeel Mestayer, Julia Retzlaff and Sachiel Rosen completed a 10-day hunger strike in defense of the first and only College of Ethnic Studies (COES) in the nation under the name of the TWLF. The negotiations yielded $482,806 for the COES rather than the proposed cuts of $200,000, which had sparked the protest on May 1, 2016. The funding they won was earmarked to hire new tenure-track faculty in Africana Studies and to advance the college with the establishment of two courses in Pacific Islander Studies (Barba, 2016). Yet again, the memory of the Third World Liberation Front at San Francisco State University was revived to address an institutional attempt to cut vital resources to the COES as well as bring attention to some of the most pressing issues in the community. With the conclusion of their successful hunger strike, the 2016 TWLF articulated the connection between the proposed cuts and larger systemic issues impacting their community in the following statement:

> *Our work as a coalition is to put an end to the systemic racism that invests in the mass incarceration of our people instead of in their education. We must stand together to resist the systemic racism that has allowed murdering police forces to go unpunished. We must resist the systemic racism that has allowed the mass displacement of San Francisco's community. It is time we rise up as the people and put an end to the systematic silencing of our narratives and communities (Third World Liberation Front, 2016).*

The sentiments of the 2016 SFSU TWLF are a direct reflection of the original call to action that guided the movement for Ethnic Studies in 1968-9. They also exemplify the inherently political nature of a critical Ethnic Studies education. The reason these themes continue to emerge from those defending Ethnic Studies is because our field was established to critique and challenge the systems that have contributed to the oppression and exploitation of our communities.

My goal in providing this brief version of the history and context surrounding the creation and maintenance of Ethnic Studies is to remind the reader that Ethnic Studies was designed to be an applied praxis. Our histories cannot and should not be taught in a traditional manner. We emerged in radical opposition to the status quo, because of the systemic forces that the TWLF movement was originally fighting against (white supremacy, capitalism, state violence, racism, etc.)

still disproportionately impact our communities, our praxis must continuously respond and realign to new manifestations of these ideologies. It is not enough to study race: we must actively engage in dismantling the ideologies and systems that give race meaning. This is precisely what differentiates Ethnic Studies from other fields. *Ethnic Studies exists because it embraces the politics of education and it centralizes the responsibility of educators and students to take ownership of their relationship and the knowledge that emerges from their collaboration.*

Gauging the relevance and value of our research and community engaged scholarship based on the impact we have on people's lived experiences is the flagship of Ethnic Studies praxis. Preparing our students to apply an Ethnic Studies framework to any professional field has resulted in our alumni making important contributions in many areas of public service. Our faculty and alumna have written some of the most canonical Ethnic Studies texts, pushing forward the discourse on the intersectionality of race, gender, class, sexuality, ableism, and immigration. Graduates of our programs are now teaching at institutions across the country and mentoring other first-generation students to ensure that the youth know their presence in higher education is a political act. These students have become lawyers, community organizers, and public servants working on critical social issues of our day, like dismantling the Prison Industrial Complex, facilitating youth empowerment, and advocating for food and climate justice. The struggles and concerns in our communities, such as fighting against the inhumane treatment of immigrants, gentrification, water pollution, the ongoing policies of genocide against Indigenous peoples, and police and state violence, must continue to inform how we engage as Ethnic Studies practitioners in this political moment.

50 years of Ethnic Studies has also yielded a wealth of research that highlights the impact that the discipline has had on its students and society. Exposure to an Ethnic Studies curriculum and critical pedagogy should not be a privilege denied until higher education. It should be integrated as core curriculum to prepare young people with the tools to read the world they live in and increase their ability to organize for social justice and empathize with the experiences of people different from themselves. In addition to the research that shows how Ethnic Studies improves the social and academic outcomes of students of color (Sleeter, 2011), research by Hughes, Bigler and Levy (2007) also concludes that curriculum that explicitly teaches about racism and how to challenge it contributes to improved racial attitudes and understanding among White children. This research exemplifies the essence and great potential impact of Ethnic Studies and what it means for a discipline to embrace the politics of education.

It serves as an important reminder that teaching young people from an Ethnic Studies perspective can counter the vitriolic narratives that thrive on ignorance and fear and that permeate our society. The current state of our national and world politics requires a profound recommitment to a political education focused on the areas of social justice, climate justice and expanding true political power to the masses. I am optimistic that with the expansion of Ethnic Studies at the K-12 level, more youth will be inspired to address the urgent crises of their time and continue the legacy of Ethnic Studies as a praxis of liberation.

## References

"Afro-American Studies 1-155" Request for Approval or Withdrawal of a Course Forms University Archives Records Collection. Berkeley: The Bancroft Library, University of California, Berkeley. n.d. CU-9, Box 8282.2. Print.

Althusser, L. (1971). Lenin and philosophy, and other essays. New York: Monthly Review Press.

Anderson, J. D. (1995). The education of Blacks in the South, 1860-1935. Chapel Hill, NC: Univ. of North Carolina Press.

Barba, M. (2016, May 11). Students end hunger strike after reaching agreement with SFSU president. San Franciso Examiner. Retrieved from http://www.sfexaminer.com/students-end-hunger-strike-reaching-agreement-sfsu-president/

Blau, P. M., & Duncan, O. D. (1967). The American occupational structure. New York: Wiley.

Blauner, R. (April 01, 1969). Internal Colonialism and Ghetto Revolt. Social Problems, 16, 4, 393-408.

Bowles, S., & Gintis, H. (1976). Schooling in capitalist America: Educational reform and the contradictions of economic life. New York: Basic Books.

Delgado, Z. J. (2016). The Longue Durée of Ethnic Studies: Race, Education and the Struggle for Self-Determination.

Fanon, F. (2004). The wretched of the earth: Frantz Fannon ; with a foreword by Homi K. Bhabha and a preface by Jean-Paul Sartre. New York: Grove Press.

Fischer, C. S. (1996). Inequality by design: Cracking the bell curve myth. Princeton, N.J: Princeton university press.

hooks, b. (1994). Teaching to transgress: Education as the practice of freedom. New York: Routledge.

Hughes, J. M., Bigler, R. S., & Levy, S. R. (November 01, 2007). Consequences of Learning About Historical Racism Among European American and African American Children. Child Development, 78, 6, 1689-1705.

Johnson, G. T. (June 06, 2008). Constellations of Struggle: Luisa Moreno, Charlotta Bass, and the Legacy for Ethnic Studies. Aztlan: a Journal of Chicano Studies, 33, 1, 155-172.

Lee, R. E. (2012). The longue durée and world-systems analysis. New York: State University of New York Press.

O'Donnell, J., Pruyn, M., & Chávez, R. C. (2004). Social justice in these times. Greenwich, Conn: Information Age Pub.

Prashad, V. (2007). The darker nations: A people's history of the third world. New York: New Press.

Sleeter, C. E., & National Education Association. (2011). The Academic and Social Value of Ethnic Studies: A Research Review.

Third World Liberation Front. (2016, May 8). Update: SFSU Hunger Strike for Ethnic Studies demands that negotiations begin immediately. San Francisco Bay View. Retrieved from http://sfbayview.com/2016/05/sf-state-hunger-striker-hassani-bell-speaks-on-cuts-to-ethnic-studies-and-aims-of-their-movement/

Third World Strike at University of California, Berkeley collection, CES ARC 2015/1 Ethnic Studies Library, University of California, Berkeley. Location: 1.71 TWLF box 1 Folder 71 1969 - Publications pamphlets. p. 4.

Uncatalogued TWLF archive UC Berkeley. (2016). Course Catalogue "1970 Ethnic Studies."

Uncatalogued TWLF archive UC Berkeley. (2016). Course Catalogue "Department of Ethnic Studies, 1979-1980."

Woodson, C. G. (1933). The mis-education of the Negro. http://www.historyisaweapon.com/defcon1/misedne.html#NOT7

# BSU/TWLF Veterans Support Arab American Studies (April 2020)

Fifty years ago, as members of the Black Student Union (BSU) and the Third World Liberation Front (TWLF) of SF State and TWLF of UC Berkeley; we conducted the longest student strikes in US history to open educational institutions up to our histories, our cultures, and our communities as racially oppressed peoples. Out of this historic strike emerged the field of Ethnic Studies. As veterans of the BSU and the TWLF who sacrificed to breathe life into Ethnic Studies, we stand solidly behind the inclusion of Arab American Studies in California's Ethnic Studies Model Curriculum

While the main protagonists within the TWLF were African Americans, Asian Americans, Latinas/os, and Native Americans, the spirit of the TWLF encompassed all those struggling against racism and colonialism. Arab and Muslim activists participated in and expressed solidarity with the TWLF strike. Both the Organization of Arab Students (OAS) and the Iranian Student Association (ISA) actively and unconditionally supported the goals of the SFSU strike in particular, and, the goal of decolonizing the curriculum in general. OAS and ISA shared BSU/TWLF opposition to the Vietnam war with the same unequivocal commitment to opposing US intervention in the Middle East and elsewhere.

The destiny of Arab and Muslim students is intimately intertwined with our struggles. This was our commitment in 1968 and it remains our commitment today, as our histories illustrate. In California, we are slowly (and gratefully) recognizing that the United Farm Workers included Filipino and Yemeni workers as well as Mexican workers. The names of UFW founders Philip Vera Cruz and Larry Itliong now proudly stand alongside Cesar Chavez and Dolores Huerta. This history of struggle in the fields is even richer when we acknowledge that thousands of Yemeni laborers joined the fight for labor rights and dignity. The names of Arab Yemeni UFW organizers must now be learned by students in California schools to offer our students a more comprehensive education and tell the rich stories of our communities. The story of Nagi Daifallah, a young Yemeni organizer who was killed by a Kern County sheriff in 1973 as he defended Cesar Chavez must be taught to students to tell a more fuller history and to allow students of Arab origin to claim pride in their histories. The role of Saeed Mohammed Al-Alas and Ahmed Shaibi must be included in the valiant history of UFW along with Cesar Chavez, Dolores Huerta, Philip Vera Cruz, Larry Itliong, to prevent part of that history from being erased.

These histories and solidarities between Indigenous, Black and Brown people, including Arabs and Muslims form the heartbeat of Ethnic Studies. They are timely and essential today as Islamophobia and anti-Arab racism become part and parcel of white supremacy, anti-Black racism and xenophobia and anti-immigrant violence. Understanding the Muslim ban alongside the caging of children and ICE raids offers a comparative lens through which Ethnic Studies has exemplified how to teach about the indivisibility of justice and the need for mutual understanding, dignity and respect. Imagining what it must feel like for Yemeni children whose parents are killed in indiscriminate bombings brings home the reality of Vietnamese, Central American, and Haitian kids and allows the student body to identify with one another. We must draw lessons of history from the 1968 strike as well as more recent times to bring our communities together, and confront legacies of hate, segregation, racism and ignorance. We note the messages of Jews of conscience who stood outside ICE and said, "Never Again for Anyone," as we learn from the Japanese community that demanded last summer not to repeat history. We are equally inspired by our members from Student Non-Violent Coordinating Committee (SNCC) who drew on their lunch counter experiences and boycotts in the Jim Crow South and South African anti-Apartheid youth. In 1968, Martin Luther King, Jr. affirmed that justice is indivisible. In 2018, Angela Davis wrote, freedom is a constant struggle. As the murals honoring our struggles adorn our campuses, they remind us of how linked our lived experiences are and what we fought for in 1968.

As veterans of the student strike at San Francisco State and University of California, Berkeley, we stand solidly in support of the inclusion of Arab American Studies as part of the California Ethnic Studies Model Curriculum. It is a logical extension of what we fought for so many years ago: a relevant and liberatory education that will lead to a different world.

# An Ethnic Studies Movement Across California As Never Before

*R. TOLTEKA CUAUHTIN*

Left: January 2019. Tolteka on strike with United Teachers Los Angeles at Yangna (Los Angeles) City Hall. (Right) Save CA Ethnic Studies Coalition poster, August 2019. Created in response to attacks from outside communities of color, against the Ethnic Studies Model Curriculum draft.. Image by Steven Krieg Acevedo.

## Save CA Ethnic Studies Coalition - Our Hxstorical Context

Sometimes when you get hit, you come back stronger and in more solidarity, than ever; the Save CA Ethnic Studies Coalition knows this - it was born out of this struggle. Attacks against Ethnic Studies (ES) are nothing new; they have been occurring for 52 plus years, and more specifically for more than 520 years upon this continent. Ethnic Studies was alive and well in the Gregorian year of 1491, thriving across: Abya Yala (Turtle Island and Tawantinsuyo; Ixachilan; the Americas), Alkebulan (Africa), Asia, Oceania – literally, all the continents where communities of color and Native peoples originate from. Today, in the Gregorian year 2020 (though our ancestral calendars are much older) – ES is alive. Ethnic Studies is regenerating, growing, while still struggling to exist in the state level institutions in the ways we as communities of color and Native peoples ourselves determine, define, and give knowledge and life to, for our past, present, and future generations.

With the advent of European colonialism, the invention of whiteness and global white supremacist culture began, along with the criminalization and attacks against us and our people of color centered worldviews and knowledge. Our epistemologies (knowledge systems), languages, pedagogical (teaching) and curricular traditions, were outlawed, displaced, stolen, and co-opted by (neo)colonial Eurocentric traditions. This is a centuries old part of what educational scholar Gloria Ladson-Billings calls the education debt: the cultural-historical, sociopolitical, economic, and moral debt the United States and California still owe communities and students of color today. This manifests itself through the pervasive opportunity gap, or so-called achievement gap impacting our schools and students today. The impact of this debt has continued throughout centuries, in multiple forms. Still, we did not perish, nor did our worldviews and knowledge. We continue to evolve in struggle – our current Save CA Ethnic Studies movement is a testament to this – History, Herstory...

Our story, connecting our millennial roots since time immemorial, to 528 years ago, through to just 52 years ago and since, bridging today to tomorrow in the spiral of spacetime. On the ancestral lands of the Tongva, Tataviam, and Chumash – in East Los Angeles, Southern California, and as part of the Chicano (Chicana / Xicanx) Movement, students organized, mobilized, and walked out of five East LA high schools. One of their demands was to see our peoples and knowledge reflected in the otherwise biased, Eurocentric, and traumatizing K-12 school curriculum. Later that Goregorian year, 1968, at San Francisco State University on the ancestral lands of the Ohlone, and in solidarity with the Black Student Union there, a new coalition emerged for that moment, the Third World Liberation Front (TWLF). The TWLF also demanded to see our peoples and knowledge in the institution's curriculum; soon after, the TWLF movement spread and sparked up a chapter UC Berkeley, also on Ohlone land - and bringing student activism to campuses in CA as never before.

By 1969 students of color were organizing and leading the two longest student strikes in all of US history at these two universities, even when attacked by the National Guard who was sent in by California Governor Regan — and even as many students were arrested for taking a stand for their education. The TWLF movement persisted through those oppressive moments, while the state of CA and Governor Reagan chose to be on the wrong side of history and the wrong side of the education debt yet again. The student activists did not give up though, in solidarity together, and the first College of Ethnic Studies (at SF State) and Department of Ethnic Studies (at UCB) in California, were founded as a direct result of this student organizing and activism. Originals/veteranxs student strikers from then, 50 years ago, are now part of our Save CA Ethnic Studies movement in support of the Ethnic Studies Model Curriculum draft.

## Save CA Ethnic Studies Coalition - Today

Will Ethnic Studies communities have to walk out, sit in, boycott, rally, protest, and take other direct actions for a course that carries the name Ethnic Studies (ES) at the CA state level in 2021? We will see...

## Who Are We?

We're part of a statewide movement that is connecting Ethnic Studies communities across the state as never before, a diverse coalition of all races and a multiplicity of ethnicities, intergenerationally connected, geographically spread, continuing a 50+ year legacy of student, educator, and community activism for this critical cause. The coalition, and its supporting organizations, have combined memberships of over 500,000 people. The movement is directly related to California Assembly Bill 2016, which was signed into law encouraging all California high schools to offer Ethnic Studies and asks the California Department of Education (CDE) to develop a model curriculum as an optional guide–rather than as a mandate such as the K-12 Eurocentric state standards (1998) – for these courses.

In November of 2018, a core of 20 Ethnic Studies educator leaders were selected by the CA Instructional Quality Commission (IQC) and appointed by the State Board of Education (SBE) to serve on the Ethnic Studies Model Curriculum Advisory Committee (ES-MCAC). From February-April of 2019, in three sessions (2 days each), the expert committee did its work with extremely limited time, parameters, and public comments. Revisions were made based on committee members' knowledge of the field/discipline of Ethnic Studies and its community of color group specific fields; and based on their collective thousands of hours of curriculum development and classroom teaching experience. Both in February and April, the committee asked for more time to do its work, and to be as thorough as necessary for this new state-level curriculum called Ethnic Studies - this time extension was denied the educators..

Thus, in May of 2019, the CA IQC, approved the draft for the next stage of public comments, with only minor revisions. All was going well and low-key for over a month, including with support from leading K-20 Ethnic Studies scholars and educators, including Christine Sleeter, who wrote the only piece of literature specifically cited in AB2016 legislation, the National Education Association review of K-12 Ethnic Studies, which several districts also cited in passing their Ethnic Studies graduation requirements. The public comment process was going smooth until mid-summer 2019, when boom! A blitz from different realms of whiteness hit the CDE, ESMC and Ethnic Studies communities hard.

## What Happened & Who Attacked? White Privilege, Implicit Bias, & The Status Quo Keepers

This particular stage of the movement and coalition emerged when attacks *from outside communities of color* came against the Ethnic Studies Model Curriculum (ESMC) draft in July and August 2019. These attacks put intense and immense pressure on the California Department of Education and caused them to have a rushed and reactionary response that unfortunately did not consult or consider communities of color at all - seemingly falling into a trap of institutional racism for the time being, yet again. We as Ethnic Studies communities, had a decision to make, give up or fight back with the legacy of activism we inherited.

Specifically, there were five fronts, all from outside communities of color, that the attacks against the ESMC draft came from in August 2019. These whitestream attacks came from a) biased white-dominant corporate establishment media (cem) op-ed pages, b) explicitly racist right-wing white nationalists who do not want Ethnic Studies to exist at all (Breitbart being one of their cem arms), c) climate crisis denying conservatives who want the educational system failing students of color and oppressive world to stay the same (Wall Street Journal, one of their cem arms), d) "white moderates/faux liberals/neoliberals" who the late great Martin Luther King Jr. warned about, who may say they support Ethnic Studies with their words, yet act in implicitly racist paternalistic ways, signaling their deeper sentiment that they only support ES if it's done in the way and with the language they as the all-knowing white moderates/neoliberals think best—while using right-wing talking points (their cem arms, LA Times Op-Ed pages, SF Chronicle, etc.), and lastly, e) the Israel Lobby and CA Legislative Jewish Caucus, because of the inclusion of an Arab American Studies course in the ESMC and specifically the inclusion of the Boycott, Divestments, and Sanctions movement, from the Palestinian perspective in the curriculum; as well as a desire for the curriculum to be more inclusive of the Jewish experience. Then and now, there are many white allies and Jewish allies in solidarity with the Save CA Ethnic Studies movement, and in support of the ESMC's overall original draft. Revisions are part of the process, the original advisory committee had certain requests for revisions that were not granted; all of these large scale wholesale attacks against the ESMC (rather than reasonable requests for certain revisions), were largely explicitly and implicitly racist.

Because of the pressure upon the CDE and their reactionary response in August, in Ethnic Studies communities, there was a great concern that this state level of Ethnic Studies could now be converted into a very superficial version for the model curriculum, more along the lines of multicultural or diversity studies. The discipline of Ethnic Studies itself was in danger being completely reframed and removed of its transformative potential at the high school level — again silencing Ethnic Studies communities of color and harming students of color in the process, further concretizing the centuries old, cultural-historical, sociopolitical, economic, and moral education debt, rather than addressing it as needs to be done for this statewide project, the first of its nature in the entire country.

50+ years after Governor Reagan sent the National Guard in against Ethnic Studies students, we are still dealing with these explicitly and implicitly racist attacks. California as a state is supposed to be better than this in 2020 and not cave into pressures from whiteness and the alt-right hegemonic white alliance, including the white moderate/neoliberal attack on the framing and academic language of the curriculum. Caving to these pressures equating to institutional racism, is especially the case for a project that is designed to serve communities of color at the core, and directly address the education debt in all its facets, rather than reifying and reinforcing it. That would be a hijacking, continuing the marginalization of communities of color, and silencing Ethnic Studies teachers of color in the process. Should we accept that possibility and be complacent with it?

## 50+ Years of Ethnic Studies Activism Rises Again - The Legacy Continues

Something had to be done at that moment, Ethnic Studies communities had to come together to defend it... in defense of ES! Thus, the Save CA Ethnic Studies movement was catalyzed, announced by the LA Times newsroom (not their op-ed pages) on August 21st, 2019, had its first press conference on August 26th, 2019 and launched a petition on September 4th that had gained over 10,000 grassroots signatures in less than a month, and over 100 intersectional community based organizations, associations, institutions and units in support.

Though the controversy and attacks against the curriculum from outside communities of color received most of the mainstream media attention back then, the overall strength of the document within the context of Ethnic Studies, and the vast support within communities of color quickly became evident. Soon enough, the grassroots community power of the Save CA Ethnic Studies movement was undeniable. By the CA Instructional Quality Commission meeting on September 20th, 2019, it was clear the advocacy had an impact and the discussion was changing, with both State Board of Education and Instructional Quality Commission members sharing words of appreciation and support for the advisory committee, and the overall draft, as well as over 50 community members in support that day, representing many thousands more.

Since September 2019, the three demands/goals of the Save CA Ethnic Studies coalition are the following:

Keep the current model curriculum draft (with some revisions) focused on the histories and social justice struggles of communities of color in the U.S.

Maintain the Ethnic Studies curricular framework—with disciplinary knowledge, language, and pedagogy—by not diluting or converting it into a non-equivalent field (i.e., multicultural studies, diversity studies, or area studies).

Improve accountability, transparency, and make revisions with Ethnic Studies expert practitioners, including members of the ES-MC Advisory Committee, throughout the entire model curriculum revision process and up until its completion and ratification.

Black Lives Matter, Asian American Political Alliance, California Indian History Curriculum Coalition, Chicano Latino School Boards Association, the California Teachers Association, California Faculty Association, Cal State University Council on Ethnic Studies, and many more joined in support early on. East LA Walkout and TWLF OG's from both SF State and UC Berkeley, through to new university Ethnic Studies Student Committees, and high school students, are joined in solidarity with this movement today!

## TWLF-Save CA ES in Effect at the UC Berkeley Multicultural Center & Beyond

As part of this campaign of the last few months, over a five day span in October 2019, I had the honor of helping coordinate and present at an event at the UCB Multicultural Center with Save CA Ethnic Studies TWLF OG's and high school student activists, a few hours after landing in the Bay from Yangna (LA). It was student strike veterana Vicci Wong who linked me up with Christine Hong, director of Critical Race and Ethnic Studies at UC Santa Cruz, and who helped bring this NorCal Save CA ES speaking tour together.

On our interactive panel that day were TWLF striker Harvey Dong, who also happens to be the owner of the Eastwind Bookstore in Berkeley (the publisher of this brave book), and veteranxs Clementina Duron, Nina Genera, and Maria Ramirez, all strong TWLF members for 50+ years and still active and dedicated to the struggle. We were joined by UCB ES Coordinator and Professor Keith Feldman, UCB ES PhD candidate and activist Marcelo Felipe Garzo Montalvo, Oakland and Emory high school students Sariah Hill, Ne'Jahra Soriano, and Youth Together organizer, Meesh Cabral. Multiracial and intergenerational solidaridad together in action and to help Save CA Ethnic Studies, what an experience!

That night I took a train to UC Davis to get ready for the next day. There, I linked up with Robyn Rodriguez, chair of Asian American Studies and founder of the Bulosan Center for Filipino Studies, for a couple presentations, took a tour of their Ethnic Studies department, and found out that students also went on strike at UCD 50 years ago for Ethnic Studies. This was another great experience and strengthening of the movement. Within a couple days, I was back in the Bay at SF State for their TWLF ES 50th Commemoration Week. Here again, I was able to connect with BSU/TWLF OG's Ramona Tascoe - who has been with us in strong solidarity since August, and Danny Glover, who though you may be familiar with his name and classic flicks, you may not know he was also an original SF State TWLF member and student striker 52 years back. I also had the honor of joining a panel for the Cal State University Council on Ethnic Studies at SF State that weekend, with leaders in the field, and we are thankful the CSU Council on ES has been in solidarity with us since August 2019 as well - la lucha sigue!

## We Are Ethnic Studies - What's Your Part of This Story?

This story is far from done; now you have a better idea of where it comes from and where it's at, and you yourself—as a general reader, Ethnic Studies community member, and/or in an Ethnic Studies class this very moment—are connecting to it. We are still struggling for Ethnic Studies after five decades/centuries. What will the future hold for our struggle and story? How will you connect to the story? Reading this booklet is a start. Connecting to your local Ethnic Studies community is a next step, and whenever you'd like to loop in to the state and national level work, here we are. Save CA Ethnic Studies! Community and People Power! In Lak Ech! TWLF/Ethnic Studies Onward - the legacy continues!

# Save CA Ethnic Studies Photos

R. TOLTEKA CUAUHTIN

Sacramento, April 2019; the Ethnic Studies Model Curriculum Advisory Committee and Writers, including leading Ethnic Studies educators in the state and world, along with then Executive Director of the California Instructional Quality Commission (and as of March 2020, Chief Deputy Superintendent) Stephanie Gregson, and CDE Consultant Ken McDonald.

In July and August 2019, the right wing and corporate establishment media attack the Ethnic Studies Model Curriculum, and it blow it up nationally - as shown here through several headlines. And with such intense and immense pressure, the CDE does whatever it can to calm it.... however, this jeopardizes the Ethnic Studies integrity, of the whole project.

*August 14, 2019, at the CDE, the State Superintendent of Public Instruction, Tony Thurmond, hosted a joint press conference with CA Jewish Legislative Caucus representatives. While at the press conference, the Superintendent refuted charges that the curriculum is anti-Semitic—he also indicated that Ethnic Studies at the high school level and this curriculum, could shift its focus away from communities of color and diverge from the higher education model of the field. In other words, the discipline itself and the legacy of Ethnic Studies was all of a sudden in jeopardy because of attacks from outside.*

*By August 21st, the Save CA Ethnic Studies Coalition emerges and is announced by the LA Times newsroom, bringing forth many of the coalition's concerns to the world. Note: LA Times newsroom who announced the Save CA Ethnic Studies Coalition is more fair, and distinct from the implicitly racist LA Times "moderate" op-ed writers who took a more whitesplaining approach in its explanation on what Ethnic Studies should be.*

*Above: At the first Save CA Ethnic Studies press conference in Yangna (Los Angeles) on August 26th, 2019, local Ethnic Studies students, educators, and leaders gather. From left to right in this foreground of this picture, high school student Mayan Goldberg (daughter of CTA Vice President David Goldberg), Black Lives Matter LA lead and Cal State Los Angeles Professor of Pan-African Studies, Melina Abdullah, United Teachers Los Angeles Ethnic Studies representative and Association of Raza Educators Los Angeles Chair Lupe Carrasco Cardona, and Jack McNair scholar and UCLA Ethnic Studies Student Committee representative, Brian Zamora - intergenerationally and multiracially, all in solidarity for the Ethnic Studies Model Curriculum (ESMC).*

Above: Bay Area Save CA Ethnic Studies Press Conference including participation by SFUSD Board members, teacher leaders. Present at this event were ESMC Adv Committee members/writers Allyson Tintiangco-Cubales, Artnelson Concordia, Aimee Riechel and others.

Top: San Diego Save CA Ethnic Studies Teacher Leader and ESMC Advisory Committee writer, Guillermo Gomez, along with Assembly and Instructional Quality Commission member Dr. Shirley Weber, and 9th grade Ethnic Studies students at Lincoln High School in SDUSD. Bottom: Student organization, Afro-Latinx Connection, part of the UCLA Ethnic Studies Student Committee, formed as part of the Save CA Ethnic Studies campaign, in September 2019. Right: Save CA ES circle logo by Eunice Ho.

*Following photos: Save CA Ethnic Studies Coalition supporters attend the IQC meeting in Sacramento, with TWLF OG's and Ethnic Studies leaders, and submit a petition of over 8,000 signatures gathered in less than 3 weeks. There are many affirmations from both Instructional Quality Commission and State Board of Education members that day, September 20th, 2019.*

*Save CA Ethnic Studies - UCB TWLF OG Presentation to a full room at the Cal Multicultural Community Center on October 8th, 2019, from left to right: TWLF veteranxs Harvey Dong, Maria Ramirez, Nina Genera, Save CA ES Statewide Liaison R. Tolteka Cuauhtin, Oakland high school student Sariah Hill, Youth Together organizer Meesh Cabral, Emory high school student Ne'Jahra Soriano, and UC Berkeley Department of Ethnic Studies Coordinator and Professor, Keith Feldman.*

# Ethnic Studies Historical Legacy

*MARIA E. RAMIREZ AND NINA GENERA*

*Maria E. Ramirez and Nina Genera were the first entering Chicano Studies students after the TWLF strike of 1969. In picture, they are attending TWLF 50th commemoration, holding signs that demand establishment of a College of Ethnic Studies at UC Berkeley. January 22, 2019. Harvey Dong photo.*

Beginning in 1492, when the European nations came to claim different parts of this hemisphere as theirs, first as New Spain, then later as New England, New France, New Netherlands, etc., the land was not empty, Indigenous nations, peoples inhabited and were thriving here. The Colonizers quickly brought, stole, enslaved, Africans to our lands in huge numbers. Early on, the Spanish colonizers also kidnapped, tricked almost 200,000 Chinese to Cuba alone.

Over time, the nation called the United States of America emerged out of multiple colonial wars in 1776. This nation continued its westward expansion, thru wars of aggression and extermination and annexation, forming the current boundaries of the country we see today that include Alaska, Hawaii, and the Island of Puerto Rico.

From its inception, the eyewitnesses, to this nation building on up to the present times, are Native American, Chicano/ Latino, African Americans and

Asian Americans. The continuing historical marginalization of these groups in particular, served as a rallying call for Ethnic Studies back in 1969.

50 years ago, the Third World Liberation Front, first at San Francisco State, then at UC Berkeley, challenged the sole narrative of Eurocentric Education, aka White Supremacy/nationalism. The demands for Ethnic Studies was, and is in truth, academic liberation of our minds, and honors the shared, intertwined histories and perspectives of these groups in the formation of this nation.

In 2019, 50-year commemorations of the student led strikes, brought together veterans of the strikes, along with all the following generations of students, staff, that fought to strengthen the program, when the University's sought to downsize, minimize, erase us. They continue to support and expand on the original vision of self-determination, student centered, community based, Third World College. The momentum for Ethnic Studies continues and has our full support for the passage of Ethnic Studies in California high Schools, again focusing on the 4 main groups at the foundational level of this nation.

We remind Academia that 524 years after Columbus so called discovery, in 1492, of the islands off the coast of America, the European version taught in the educational system is being challenged now more than ever. The federal holiday called Columbus Day, is being reclaimed, to Indigenous Peoples day, more and more, in large part due to the teaching of Ethnic Studies., which also ties in Columbus bringing slavery and genocide to the America's.

1519 to 2019, marks the 500 commemoration of the arrival on the continent's mainland of Hernan Cortez with his men with guns and men in robes. Driven by "The Doctrine of Discovery", the lands claimed by Spain extended from Mexico up the eastern coast to Florida and beyond, and on up to the Pacific Northwest. Spain effectively detribalized a huge percentage of the indigenous people they colonized with Spanish surnames, Spanish language, and Spanish religion. In New Spain, both Native and African were enslaved. The colonial and national wars continually changed boundaries, the most expansive being the war of 1846-1848 with Mexico, just 25 years after independence from Spain, Chicanos, Mexicanos, Latinos fell under the new borders, and governance of the United States of America.

African Americans in particular are highlighting this year 1619-2019, as the 400 year commemoration, of the founding of Jamestown and more specifically, bringing Africans with them at the beginning of their settlement. Thus began, the start of the wars, treaties relocations, massacres with the native nations and the growing slave trade in this part of the America's under Anglo American governance, This original colony of New England, grew to 13 colonies, that then broke away from their colonial power, becoming the newly formed United States of America in 1776. The westward expansion continued and following the Mexican American war, and the Civil War, the US started the importation of Chinese laborers ,increasing to tens of thousands of Chinese to exploit in the building of the transcontinental railway By 1875, the first Chinese Exclusion act banning Chinese women from immigrating here, went into effect, followed by full out ban on all Chinese coming here in 1882. The first law banning members of a specific ethnic group from immigrating here.

2019 also marks the 100th commemoration of the passage of Women's Suffrage in the houses of Congress of the United States in 1919. Only white women received the right to vote, even though African American women pushed for Suffrage and women's rights, as they had been the victims of racial and gender violence during and post slavery. Native women that had flourished and were protected, valued, under the Clan Mothers, lost all rights under White male patriarchy. The institutionalization of European Patriarchy, with its hierarchal social structure began with colonization. This form of Patriarchy is highly misogynistic, racist and gender intolerant, anti Semitic, and objectifies the Earth, in the name of profit. Ethnic Studies provides the validation and opportunity for the decolonizing voices of Women and men of color to challenge the White male Patriarchal hierarchy that began in 1492.

In closing, although Ethnic Studies courses, programs and departments continue their presence in many institutions of higher education, few have been given academic credibility with validity to become institutionalized into the mainstream of academia. The California Department of Education has a responsibility to our high school students to institutionalize Ethnic Studies programs within its curriculum. It has been derelict for the past 50 years in providing more inclusivity within its subjects, short of adding Caesar Chavez here and Maya Angelou there in classroom, curricula or publisher textbooks. The participation and influence of Native American, Chicanx/Latinx, African American, Asian American run so deep in the development and shaping of our country across the curricula, in history, culture, social and labor movements, fine arts and literature, sciences and mathematics, sports, and all other realms. Ethnic Studies courses in our high schools strengthens learning and achievement and is liberating.

# Appendix

# Chronology of Events

*ABRAHAM RAMIREZ*

## JANUARY 1968

Tet Offensive in Vietnam, Viet Cong temporarily seized the US embassy in Saigon. This marked a turning point as the American public increasingly disapproved of the war.

## MARCH 3, 1969

More than 1,000 Chicano students walk out of Abraham Lincoln High School in L.A. in protest of school conditions. The student strike known as the East Los Angeles Blowouts would later have over 10,000 high school students walk out by the end of the week. Demands included Mexican American studies textbooks and curriculum, hiring of Mexican American teachers and administrators, community control of education, and improvements in cafeteria and library facilities.

## MARCH 16, 1968

My Lai Massacre was the mass murder of 347 to 504 unarmed citizens of Vietnam, mostly women and children, by US Army forces on in the hamlets of My Lai and My Khe during the Vietnam War. Many of the victims were raped, beaten, tortured, or mutilated. The incident prompted widespread outrage around the world and reduced US support at home for the war in Vietnam.

## MARCH 1968

SF State Third World Liberation Front (TWLF) was formed with the Black Students Union (BSU), the Mexican American Student Confederation (MASC), the Philippine American Collegiate Endeavor (PACE), the Intercollegiate Chinese for Social Action (ICSA), the Latin American Students Organization (LASO), and the Native American Students Union (NASU). The Asian American Political Alliance (AAPA) joined the TWLF by summertime. A member of PACE was elected as the TWLF's first chairperson.

## APRIL 4, 1968

Assassination of Martin Luther King Jr. His murder was followed by urban riots nationwide in up to 76 cities.

## APRIL 6, 1968

Bobby Hutton, 16 years old and the first Black Panther Party recruit, was killed in Oakland during a police raid of the BPP headquarters.

## MAY 1968

Asian American Political Alliance (AAPA) was formed in Berkeley and San Francisco. TWLF at SF State staged a sit-in at President Summerskill's office, which resulted in the opening of 412 admission slots for TW applicants over the next two semesters and the creation of at least 10 faculty positions for TW positions. Sit-in also involved first major act of police violence against student demonstrators with clubbings, ten injuries requiring hospitalization, and twenty-six arrests. Summerskill resigned a few months later, and there was no fulfillment of earlier agreements. Student frustration lead to divergence from traditional protest channels.

Asian American Political Alliance (AAPA) was formed in Berkeley and San Francisco. SF State TWLF staged a sit-in at President Summerskill's office, which resulted in the opening of 412 admission slots for TW applicants over the next two semesters and the creation of at least 10 faculty positions for TW positions. Sit-in also involved first major act of police violence against student demonstrators with clubbings, ten injuries requiring hospitalization, and twenty-six arrests. Summerskill resigned a few months later, and there was no fulfillment of earlier agreements. Student frustration lead to divergence from traditional protest channels.

**1968 (April).** The Afro American Student Union (AASU) submits a proposal for a Department of African American Studies to UC Berkeley Chancellor Roger W. Heyns. In August 1968, African American scholar Dr. Andrew Billingsley is appointed to assist the Chancellor in developing the African American Studies Department. In November, AASU representatives are asked by the Chancellor to revise the proposal three times. The proposal is then referred to the College of Letters and Science (L&S) for review. L&S then refers the proposal to its Executive Committee, which in turn met and revised the proposal with numerous deletions. The deletions affected the proposal's important aspects of community orientation, fieldwork and student participation. The L&S Executive Committee questioned whether it would become a department or should exist only as a "program."

**1969.** Following the formation of the Third World Liberation Front (TWLF) at San Francisco State University (SFU), the movement to establish a Third World college extends into the UC Berkeley campus when the Afro-American Students Union (AASU) approached the Asian American Political Alliance (AAPA) and the Mexican-American Student Confederation (MASC). The Native American Students United (NASU) joins the coalition days prior to the launch of TWLF's first student strike. The following 10 weeks of strike activity (January 22, 1969 to March 14, 1969) included 155 arrests, the use of riot police, the national guard, and extensive use of tear gas until a strike moratorium was called.

On March 4, 1969, the Academic Senate votes 550 to 4 to establish an interim Department of Ethnic Studies with continued negotiations for the Third World College. On March 14, 1969, strike activities cease when President Hitch authorizes the UC campus wide establishment of the Ethnic Studies Department that will confer degree programs beginning Fall 1969 in African American Studies (AAS) Asian Studies (AS), Chicano Studies (CS), and Native American Studies (NAS).

In the following week on March 20, SFSU's TWLF strike comes to an end with the establishment of the first Ethnic Studies school (later college) in the nation.

To meet high demand for courses and community engagement; students, graduate students and staff combine efforts to create new syllabi, courses and community-based programs in the surrounding Bay Area communities. An Asian Studies Field Office is established in SF Manilatown which is used as a community classroom and community center.

**1972.** Chancellor Albert Bowker fires African American Studies program coordinator Ron Lewis, charging him with "incompetence" among a list of other accusations: Bowker hires a replacement coordinator of his own choosing. In response, twenty-five African American Studies faculty sign a letter to the Chancellor asserting: "the action flagrantly violates a basic departmental prerogative in matters of internal governance." Another letter signed by twenty-five instructors is sent to the newly hired coordinator to protest and disapprove his hiring.

**1974.** The Collins Committee, a UCB review committee investigates the progress of Ethnic Studies and recommends elimination of the community engagement component. Following the review, Ethnic Studies becomes more institutionalized eliminating students in departmental operations.

African American Studies at UCB leaves the interim Ethnic Studies Department and joins L&S. In protest, student groups, including African American students, calls for a boycott of the new African American Studies department classes.

Meanwhile, SF State College establishes a School of Ethnic Studies with departments in Asian American Studies, Black Studies, La Raza Studies, and American Indian Studies. The School of Ethnic Studies shortly evolves into a College of Ethnic Studies, the first and only such college in the nation.

**1975.** The Ethnic Studies Department at UCB establishes a Comparative Ethnic Studies (CES) Program that would provide a comparative framework to study race and ethnicity. Asian to establish CES, resources are drawn from Asian American Studies (AAS), Chicano Studies (CS), and Native American Studies (NAS) reallocate funds to the establishment of CES.

**1984.** The Ethnic Studies PhD graduate program in Ethnic Studies at UCB is established. It is the first interdisciplinary PhD program in the U.S. dedicated to the study of comparative race and ethnicity in national, hemispheric, and global contexts.

**1995.** The interim Ethnic Studies Department remains in limbo, is underfunded and pressured to enter into L&S. Ethnic Studies faculty agreed to enter L&S with the reasoning that it will achieve more program support. Unresolved still is the direction of its three programs: CES, AAS, CS, and NAS. Discussion is raised to establish an Ethnic Studies Division within L&S where Asian American, Chicano and Native American Studies are departments within an overall Ethnic Studies division. The inclusion of African American Studies is considered but opposition outside academics removes this avenue.

**1996.** California Proposition 209, an anti-affirmative action measure, passes as a constitutional amendment to California constitution prohibiting public institutions from discriminating on basis of race, sex, or ethnicity.

**1998.** UC Regent Ward Connerly conducts private investigation of Ethnic Studies in the UC system to determine whether the courses have political bias and lack substance. Graduate students from UCB African American Studies and Ethnic Studies form a graduate student cooperative to oppose Ward Connerly's press attacks. A conference at UC Berkeley is hosted with a turnout of 500 attendees to defend the academic relevance of Ethnic Studies and African American Studies programs.

**1998.** Severe cutbacks in Ethnic Studies and African American Studies lead department chairs to propose that Ethnic Studies and African American Studies merge with American Studies to form a unit (possibly a division) within L&S. This proposal is strongly opposed by American Studies.

**1999.** After negotiations with administration, the department of ethnic studies was promised 8 FTE positions to fill vacancies and potential retires (over the course of 5 years), a research center (Center for Race and Gender), and a multicultural center (Multicultural Community Center), and a mural in Barrows Hall.

### January 2009. 40th Anniversary of the TWLF Strike at UC Berkeley.

**July 2009. UC Budget Cuts** — The University of California System announces a $750 million budget gap and calls for system wide layoffs. UC Berkeley, facing a $150 million deficit for the 2009-10 academic year, cuts faculty pay through furloughing workers, laying off employees, reducing course offerings, and raising student fees.

**2009. Ethnic Studies External Review** — From the many recommendations made by the outside committee for the Ethnic Studies (ES) department, among the more notable were: stronger inter-program collaboration, graduate student mentorship and funding, and recommendation for more FTE hires in all programs. The External Review (ER) finds it not sustainable to function with 4 autonomous programs inside one department of ES. The ER committee proposes the idea to dissolve the programs into one Comparative Ethnic Studies Program in order to alleviate faculty responsibilities. Review also recommends recruiting "more fundable" grad students to limit teaching (GSI) responsibilities and increase outside funding and make the "graduate studies programs more competitive."

**September 2009. Walkouts** — Beginning on September 24, faculty, staff and students across the UC system declare Day of Action to walkout and march in protest of cuts to university budgets, staff layoffs and student fee hikes. 5,000 people gather on Sproul plaza.

**February 2010. Decolonizing the University Conference** — From February 26 to 27, a gathering commemorates the 40th anniversary of Ethnic Studies and revisits the idea of the Third World College. "The first day of the conference sought to emulate a version of a Third World College (TWC) through a combination of teach-ins, dialogue, panels, performances, film screenings, and workshops." The second day of the conference involves discussions about the ways in which the TWC is possible and discussions about the political and institutional future of ES.

Film about conference: https://vimeo.com/15729523

**2010. Symbolic Hunger Strike** — On March 3, 2010, twenty Latinx students launch a symbolic hunger strike for 10 days in protest of Arizona SB 1070 and HB 2281 (Mex-Am Studies Ban). The following day on March 4, a couple thousand UC Berkeley students march from Sproul to Oscar Grant Plaza. After the rally, a few hundred people take over the freeway and arrests are made.

**2010. First Town Hall to Address Ethnic Studies** — On October 20, La Collectiva (a collective of Ethnic Studies students and graduate students) calls for a dialogue between faculty, students, staff, and community members to discuss the future of Ethnic Studies.

**2011. Ethnic Studies Meeting with Dean Carla Hesse** — On March 3, the ES community, faculty, staff and students meet with Division of Social Science Dean, Carla Hesse, to discuss coming cuts to Ethnic Studies, African American Studies (AFRAM) and Gender Women Studies (GWS).

**2011. Operational Excellence "Organizational Simplification Committee"** — On March 4, the Division of Social Sciences under the College of Letters and Sciences orders 2.5 FTE (staff) positions to be cut from the Department of Ethnic Studies. This is done at the same time they lost 2.0 FTE (full time equivalent) staff positions due to retirements, making the number **4.5**. Under the banner of "Operational Excellence," the administration consolidates staff budget, while firing staff in Ethnic Studies (ES), African American Studies (AFRAM), and Gender and Women's Studies (GWS). The staff streamlines responsibilities due to cuts on their programs.

**March 2011. Students Deliver Letter to Faculty Meeting** — On March 7, a coalition of graduate and undergraduate students in the ES department (including representatives of all programs) disrupt a faculty meeting. They deliver a letter demanding that the faculty respond to the administration (regarding the External Review recommendations to collapse programs into one single program) with a call for departmentalization of all programs. Majority of ES faculty reject demands in letter and refuse to call for departmentalization.

**March 2011. Students Deliver Letter to Administration** — On March 27, a coalition made up of undergraduates and graduate students from ES, GWS, AFRAM deliver a letter to the administration rejecting all staff cuts. They demanded the reinstatement of staff positions and for 6 target faculty for each program, totaling up to 24 faculty.

**April 2011. Hunger Strike in Solidarity with Ethnic Studies** — On April 26, students launch a hunger strike demanding all staff be reinstated, the end of Operational Excellence, support for ACR 34 (an ES bill in CA), and that UC Berkeley publicly acknowledges the unfulfilled promise of Third World College.

**April - May 2011. Ethnic Studies Town Halls** — A series of "town hall" meetings occur between faculty and students to discuss the future of ES and the Third World College. Committees are formed to develop areas of ES (funding, professionalization, curriculum, etc.) but go nowhere. Most quickly dissolve during summer break. Graduate students negotiate a representative seat at the faculty meetings. They are limited to the "opening," or first half of the meeting, and asked to leave for the closing session.

**November 2011. Occupy Cal** — On November 9, after the UC Regents approved a 32% tuition fee increase, UC Berkeley students set up camp on Sproul Plaza and occupy the space 24/7.

Video Link: https://www.youtube.com/watch?v=B_f06VQOkI4

**November 2011. Wheeler Occupation** — On November 20, a group of UC Berkeley undergraduate and graduate students occupy Wheeler Hall for an entire day demanding for those fired by UC Berkeley (mainly janitors and staff) be reinstated. Banner states "32% FEE HIKE 1900 LAYOFFS NO CLASS." Police were called in and arrests were made. Mini documentary of the Wheeler Take-Over:
 https://www.youtube.com/watch?v=ISZrR7qE-Oc

Archived sources and materials: https://reclaimuc.Blogspot.com/search?q=Ethnic+Studies

**2014. Ethnic Studies Policy Regarding Employee Kids** — The Department of ES implement a policy (that does not exist campus-wide) prohibiting ES employees from bringing children to work. A letter was delivered to Ethnic Studies chair signed by the Ethnic Studies Grad Alliance, ES Undergrad Collective, and the Grad Assembly Student Parent Advocacy Project denouncing the policy and asking for dialogue.

**2015.** Estimated $100,000 cuts are made and more in the works. Pressure by L&S for ladder rank to teach larger courses now covered by lecturers. This move leads to potentially less courses being offered.

**2016. ES Graduate Program Re-Categorized**—The Comparative Ethnic Studies Graduate Group is silently moved into the department of ES without the undergraduate or graduate student input. ES graduate students can no longer appoint African American Studies faculty as "inside" or chair dissertation committees, forcing students to appoint ES faculty as committee members in qualifying exams and dissertations.

**2016. Undergraduates Form Undergraduate 1969 Collective** — In the fall semester, an undergraduate group of primarily Chicanx/Latinx and Asian American students form the 1969 Collective as a result of wide dissatisfaction with the political orientation of the department, lack of relevant courses, cuts in course offerings, and lack of communication and transparency between faculty and undergraduate students. Students begin communication attempts with faculty.

**2016. DeCal on Palestine in ES** — In the same semester, as a result of outside (Zionist) pressure on UC Berkeley, Dean Carla Hesse suspends approval for an ES undergrad student-led class on Palestine and Settler Colonialism due to "technicalities" resulting from the course not passing through the proper curriculum oversight and approval process.

The University responded that the course did not have "sufficient degree of scrutiny to ensure that the syllabus met Berkeley's academic standards." Also stating that "It should also be noted that the Dean is very concerned about a course, even a student-run course, which espouses a single political viewpoint and/or appears to offer a forum for political organizing rather than an opportunity for the kind of open academic inquiry that Berkeley is known for."

After protests and backlash, the DeCal course on Palestine is reinstated in September.

**2017.** Further cuts in classes reduce each program (CES, AAADS, NAS and CS) to 9 classes per semester. In comparison, SFSU offers 28 Asian American Studies to 9 AAADS at UCB; 31 Latino/a American Studies classes at SFSU to 9 CS classes at UCB; 13 American Indian Studies at SFSU to 9 NAS at UCB; 23 Race and Resistance classes at SFSU to 9 CES at UCB. Also, African Studies at SFSU lists 23 classes in comparison with 29 offered in the AFRAM Department at UCB.

Staying at the program level for the remaining ethnic groups and CES within the department of ES has definitely contributed to stagnancy and demoralization. Retired faculty are not replaced. AAADS essentially has 3 tenured professors concentrated to the field of Asian American Studies and 9 part-time lecturers. In comparison, SFSU Asian American Studies has 16 tenured professors and 21 lecturers. Similar situation exists with other programs but needs more analysis.

**Fall 2017. ES Undergrad 1969 Collective Deliver Letter** — Undergraduate students march through Barrows Hall and present grievance letter to Ethnic Studies chair. Meetings between representatives of the 1969 Collective and faculty ensue throughout the semester.

**Fall 2018. ES Faculty Demand Administration Charge Students** — ES faculty submit grievance to the UC Berkeley administration demanding that students involved in the (2017) letter delivery be subjected to the student code of conduct charges. Administration rejects faculty demands.

**2018. DeCal Policy Change in ES** — Faculty in ES decide to change the DeCal course policy by establishing that there is a maximum of 2 classes and that faculty sponsors must attend 3 of the classes per sponsorship. The 2-class maximum makes it more difficult for students to find sponsors and the 3-class attendance extends a heavier workload on an already extended faculty.

**January 2019. 50th Anniversary of TWLF** — 2018-19 marks the 50th anniversary of the TWLF student strikes at SF State and UC Berkeley. TWLF veterans gather on Sproul steps rally to read the original TWLF 1969 demands. Symposium, breakout sessions and cultural performances organized at UC Berkeley. Speakers from subsequent generations who have fought to sustain Ethnic Studies on campus and in the community.

**April 2019 50th Anniversary of TWLF** — Three days of events called *Seeds of Resistance, Flowers of Liberation*.

April 24: *WHOSE UNIVERSITY?* Exhibit reception at Morrison Reading Room with panel discussion and tour.

April 25: Celebrating Community Engaged Scholarship Across Generations. Scholar activism & art practice panel, performance, and political education & pedagogy undergrad and grad panels at Anna Head Alumnae Hall.

April 26: Voices from 50 Years of Student of Color Activism. Presentation & conversation with 1969 TWLF strikers, Fannie Lou Hamer Black Resource Center, performance, and presentations on boycott and divestments from South Africa to Palestine and education in Oakland public schools at Wurster Hall.

April 27: All Power to the People. Presentation & conversation featuring 1969 TWLF strikers, presentation on Ethnic Studies beyond the university, and closing presentation featuring Decolonize this Place at Sylvia Mendez Elementary School.

**May 2020.** Scheduled launch of website: www.twLF.berkeley.edu

# Contributors

**HARVEY DONG** (editor) is a second-generation Chinese American who was active in AAPA (Asian American Political Alliance), TWLF (Third World Liberation Front) at UC Berkeley; the Asian Community Center; and the struggle to save the International Hotel. He currently teaches Asian American & Asian Diaspora Studies at UC Berkeley and is active in managing Eastwind Books of Berkeley, a community bookstore.

**JANIE CHEN** (editor) was born and raised in Oakland, CA and studies Sociology and Ethnic Studies at UC Berkeley. She works at Eastwind Books of Berkeley and is currently interning at Asian Prisoner Support Committee (APSC). Her current research involves the study of gentrification in Oakland Chinatown.

**PABLO GONZALEZ** is a first-generation Chicano scholar-activist/ anthropologist who studies the political and cultural resonance of social movements. In particular, the resonance of indigenous social movements on Chicanas/os and "people of color" in the United States. His other research interests include urban anthropology, Borderlands anthropology, decolonial thought and praxis, criminality and illegality, critical race theory/praxis, and the study of commons/enclosures. His research looks at the effects of the post 2008 Housing crisis on Latino and Black families. He is currently a continuing lecturer in Chicana/o and Latina/o Studies at UC Berkeley.

**CARLOS MUNOZ, JR.** was born in the "segundo barrio" in El Paso, Texas, and raised in the barrios of East Los Angeles, California. He is Professor Emeritus in the Department of Ethnic Studies at UC Berkeley. In 1968, he became the founding chair of the first Chicano Studies department at the California State University at Los Angeles. He is the author of numerous pioneering works on the Mexican American political experience and on African American and Latino political coalitions. After 47 years of teaching in higher education, he has gained international prominence as a political scientist, historian, journalist, and public intellectual.

**MANUEL RUBEN DELGADO** is a second generation Mexican American and Chicano activist. He was born and raised in San Bernardino, CA in the Mexican barrio known as Mt. Vernon. After dropping out of high school at the age of 16, he went on to earn a Bachelor of Arts Degree in Political Science, and in 1977, a Law Degree from UC Berkeley, and a Masters Degree in Education from San Diego State University. He is the author of the memoir, *The Last Chicano*.

**LANADA WAR JACK** is a member of the Shoshone Bannock Tribes where she lives on the Fort Hill Indian Reservation in Idaho. In January of 1968, she attended UC Berkeley and graduated in an Independent Major of Native American Law & Politics. Along with participating in the UC statewide effort in establishing Ethnic Studies programs, Dr. War Jack co-organized the takeover of Alcatraz in 1969 to end the Indian Termination Policies. She also served on various steering and executive committees of the Native American Rights Fund. Dr. War Jack is the author of *Native Resistance: An Intergenerational Fight for Survival and Life*.

**DOUG WACHTER** Born in Berkeley in 1941, Douglas Wachter grew up and was educated there, graduating from the University of California at Berkeley (UCB) with a B.A. in Biochemistry. He was the first of three boys born to parents who were intensely involved in radical politics. As a teenage boy, he was captivated by their energy and sense of purpose. At the same time, He had become fascinated by the "magic" of photography, as taught to be by his father in their home darkroom. His dual journeys as movement activist and movement photographer were destined from the start.

**YSIDRO MACIAS** is a Chicano who participated in the beginnings of the Chicano Movement in 1966, first in Los Angeles and later Berkeley/San Francisco. He was also involved in various phases of Chicano artist community. Jailed for movement activities twice. He subsequently became acquainted with Mexica dance master, Andres Segura Granados, who taught and revealed the philosophy of Aztec/Mexicas to Ysidro Macias in a 25 year friendship. Ysidro Macias previously taught at Berkeley, Merritt College, Santa Clara University, UC Irvine, Fresno City & Fresno State University, before establishing a farmworker constituency as a Fresno lawyer until 1990. He practiced law in Hawaii for a couple of years before starting the family business, now tortilla makers in the state of Hawaii.

**CLEMENTINA DURON** is a retired educator. She worked for 15 years as a bilingual teacher and 15 years as a principal in Berkeley, Oakland and San Francisco Unified School District. She graduated from UC Berkeley with a B.A. in 1971 and attended Stanford and Harvard, where she received a Masters in Education. At Lazear Elementary School, in a predominantly Mexican working class community in Oakland, herself and her parents worked closely together to create the first charter school in Oakland. She is passionate about children having equal access and opportunity in public schools.

**FLOYD HUEN** went to UC Berkeley in the late 1960s where he served as president of the Chinese Student Club and participated in the Asian American Political Alliance (AAPA) and the strike for Ethnic Studies. Huen and his wife Jean Quan co-founded the Chinatown Food Co-op and Asian Americans for Equality, a New York Chinatown-based social justice organization. In 1999, he served as the physician for the UC Berkeley hunger strikers. He is an internal medicine doctor who serves on the board of trustees for Alameda County's health system. He is also the medical director of the Over Sixties Health Center in Berkeley and Oakland.

**FRANCISCO HERNANDEZ** received his PhD and MA degrees in Education from Stanford University, a BA degree in History from UC Berkeley, and an AA degree from Sierra Junior College in California. Dr. Hernández previously served as Dean of Student Life and then as Assistant Vice Chancellor for Student Affairs at UC Berkeley. In addition to holding a number of positions in secondary and post-secondary school programs in California, Dr. Hernández also served as the Vice Chancellor of Student Affairs at the University of California, Santa Cruz, and as the Vice Chancellor for Students at the University of Hawai'i at Manoa. Dr. Hernández is recently retired and serves on several advisory committees related to increasing minority student participation in higher education.

**LILLIAN FABROS** is from Salinas, CA. She attended UC Berkeley and became a student organizer, active in the formation of the Asian Amerian Political Alliance (AAPA) and the Third World Liberation Front (TWLF). She has worked as a social worker/community organizer and attorney. Today, she is a Program Manager with Los Angeles County and volunteers in the Filipino community.

**JEFFREY THOMAS LEONG** is a poet and writer, born in Southern California and raised in the San Francisco Bay Area. For over two decades, he worked as a public health administrator and attorney for the City of San Francisco. While earning his MFA in Writing at the Vermont College of Fine Arts, he began a project to translate anew the Chinese wall poems found at the Angel Island

Immigration Station. These translations became the book Wild Geese Sorrow: The Chinese Wall Inscriptions at Angel Island published by Calypso Editions in 2018. His new book Writ, consisting of original poems also about the Angel Island detainee experience, has been published by Eastwind Books of Berkeley in March 2019.

**RICKEY VINCENT** is an Associate Professor of Diversity Studies at California College of the Arts; and lectures at UC Berkeley and City College of San Francisco. Dr. Rickey Vincent has published two books about black music, culture and politics—*Funk: The Music, the People and the Rhythm of The One* (St. Martin's Press 1996) and *arty Music: The Inside Story of the Black Panthers Band and How Black Power Transformed Soul Music* (Chicago Review Press 2013). www.rickeyvincent.com.

**LOAN DAO** is the Associate Professor and Director of Ethnic Studies at St. Mary's College of California. She earned her Ph.D. in Ethnic Studies at the University of California Berkeley and her undergraduate in Psychology, Mass Communications, and pre-law at the University of Texas at Austin. She has been active in the immigrant rights movement since the late 1990s, including co-founding one of the first national campaigns to end the deportation of Southeast Asian refugees and developing institutional changes in higher education to support undocumented, TPS, and DACA students. She formerly served as an appointee on the Massachusetts Asian American Commission and the Massachusetts Office of Refugee and Immigrants.

**ROBERTO HERNANDEZ** is an associate professor of Chicana and Chicano Studies at San Diego State University and an actively engaged, community-based researcher, scholar, teacher, and writer. Born in Mexico but raised in San Ysidro, the US/Mexico border has figured prominently in his intellectualy, political and professional development and commitments. He earned a Chicana/o Studies Honors BA, as well as Masters and PhD in Comparative Ethnic Studies from UC Berkeley.

**ULA TAYLOR** earned her doctorate in American History from UC Santa Barbara. She is the chair of the Department of African American Studies at UC Berkeley. She is the author of *The Promise of Patriarchy: Women ad the Nation.* In 2013, she received the Distinguished Professor Teaching Award for UC Berkeley, becoming the second African American woman in the history of the University to receive this award.

**JACKLIN HA** graduated from UC Berkeley in 2019 with a degree in Asian American and Asian Diaspora Studies. She is a first-generation Vietnamese American who currently works as a Youth Consultant at Banteay Srei and volunteers with BAWAR (Bay Area Women Against Rape) as a sexual assault advocate. She hopes to integrate her passion for community health in her future work as an advocate, physician, and continuing artist. Jacklin is looking forward to helping create safe spaces for youth to engage in conversations about sexual violence, trauma, and healing.

**LAILAN SANDRA HUEN** is an Oakland native and proud graduate of Oakland public schools. Huen served as OUSD's Program Manager for Asian Pacific Islander Student Achievement. She received a B.A. in Asian American Studies from Columbia University and a Master of Arts from The New School. She has worked in education and youth development for over 18 years. She has served on the Advisory Board for AYPAL: Building API Community Power and the Board of Directors for Youth Together in Oakland.

**KAI NHAM** (he/they) is a queer, trans Chinese-Vietnamese organizer. He received his B.A. in Asian American & Asian Diaspora Studies in 2019 and is pursuing his Master of Information and Data Science at the University of California, Berkeley. Holding communities at the heart of all he does, he hopes to support community work through grassroots research, technology, and design.

**JOANNE YI** graduated from UC Berkeley in 2019 with a degree in Asian American and Asian Diaspora Studies. She was the External Affairs Director and Political Advocacy Coordinator of REACH!, the UC Berkeley Asian/Pacific Islander Recruitment and Retention Center. She collaborated closely with campus and community partners in support of student-initiated recruitment and retention programs for underrepresented and underserved communities of color on campus. Joanne is currently pursuing both an MA in Education and a teaching credential in order to teach Ethnic Studies in high schools.

**RIZZA ESTACIO** graduated from UC Berkeley in 2019 with a BA in Ethnic Studies and English. While at Cal, she was the organizing director for bridges

Multicultural Resource Center, a coalition of seven recruitment and retention centers. She also served as an opinion columnist for the Daily Californian.

**ZIZA DELGADO.** Dr. Ziza Delgado Noguera is a proud critical ethnic studies practitioner and alumna of UC Berkeley where she earned her Ph.D. and M.A. in Ethnic Studies. She is an Associate Professor in Ethnic Studies at Fullerton College and conducts research on and teaches about the history of ethnic studies, race, racism, social movements, education theory and praxis, transformative justice, U.S. history, and carceral studies. Her academic and community work emphasizes the potential of education to empower historically marginalized populations. Since 2017, her campus leadership has focused on developing transformative justice programming that serves system impacted and formerly incarcerated community members on their journey to re-entry and pursuit of higher education.

**R. Tolteka Cuauhtin** is an interdisciplinary social-justice based educator, community scholar, organizer and artist. He is a statewide lead liaison and spokesperson for the Save CA Ethnic Studies Coalition, which is composed of more than a hundred community of color-based organizations and institutions. Tolteka co-chaired the California AB2016 Ethnic Studies Model Curriculum Advisory Committee in Sacramento, is on California Teachers Association/Stanford Instructional Leadership Corps, LAUSD's Ethnic Studies Teacher Leadership Team, and the Pukúu Native American Cultural Community Services Board of Directors. He has been recognized by the California State Legislature for exemplary service in meeting the needs of students of color. He also was co-founding organizer of the International Indigenous Hip Hop Gathering, and has served as education committee chair for the inaugural City of Fernando Tataviam Indigenous People's Day (IPD) Celebration.

**MARIA E. RAMIREZ** was among the first Chicano Studies students entering UC Berkeley in Fall 1969 after the TWLF strike. She has served for 30 years as a student counselor in Ohlone College. She was instrumental in assisting students and collaborating with faculty throughout her tenure by serving on various campus-wide committees, including Transfer Day, Latino Recruitment and Retention Advisory, Personal Development, Raza Day, Transfer Incentive Program, personnel selection committees, curriculum development, job fairs, career workshops, Indigenous Peoples Day events, and Women's History Month events. On August 19, 2019, the Ohlone College Board of Trustees conferred upon Maria Ramirez the title of Professor of Counseling, Personal Development, Education and Chicano Studies Emeritus of Ohlone College.

**NINA GENERA** was among the first Chicano Studies students entering UC Berkeley in Fall 1969 after the TWLF strike. Dr. Nina Genera was employed by the Ohlone College District as a Counselor/Professor from September 1976 to May 25, 2007. She was the College's first Chicana/Latina faculty member. She was originally hired as an EOPS Counselor for a one-year sabbatical replacement in the fall of 1976. She was to be dismissed after that year, but was re-hired by the Board of Trustees with the vocal support of students, parents and community. On June 13, 2012, the Ohlone College Board of Trustees conferred upon Dr. Nina Michel Genera the title of Professor of Counseling, Personal Development, Education and Chicano Studies Emeritus of Ohlone College.

**ABRAHAM RAMIREZ** is a PhD. candidate in the Department of Ethnic Studies. Abraham is interested in questions regarding migration, social movements, phenomenology, epistemology, and in general, the philosophy of race. His current and future research includes a comparative analysis of immigrant-rights activism in the US and Spain, as well as a study of the political project of ethnic studies since the 1960s. Abraham is a Chancellor's Public Fellow with the American Cultures Engaged Scholarship (ACES) and former graduate research fellow at the Center for Latino Policy Research (CLPR).

www.ingramcontent.com/pod-product-compliance
Lightning Source LLC
Chambersburg PA
CBHW081108080526
44587CB00021B/3495